Richard Strauss

Richard Strauss

David Nice

OMNIBUS PRESS
LONDON · NEW YORK · SYDNEY

For my mother

Cover design and art direction by Pearce Marchbank, Studio Twenty, London
Cover photography by Julian Hawkins

© David Nice 1993
This edition published in 1993 by Omnibus Press, a division of Book Sales Limited

Order No. OP45038
ISBN 0.7119.1686.1

Exclusive Distributors:
Book Sales Limited,
8/9 Frith Street,
London W1V 5TZ, England

Music Sales Corporation
225 Park Avenue South
New York, NY10003, USA

Music Sales Pty Ltd.,
120 Rothschild Avenue,
Rosebery, NSW 2018, Australia

To the Music Trade only:
Music Sales Limited,
8/9 Frith Street,
London WIV 5TZ, England

Typeset by Vitaset, Paddock Wood, Kent

Printed and bound in the United Kingdom by
BPCC Wheatons Limited, Exeter, Devon

A catalogue for this book is available from the British Library

Contents

MUNICH:

Munich in the late-nineteenth
century.

Chapter 1

A Classical Upbringing

Munich, the birthplace of Richard Strauss, has always had something of a reputation as an easy-going city. To the north-German sensibilities of Thomas Mann's Antonie Buddenbrooks, there was a curious absence of social distinction and a demoralising languor in the Munich air – 'the air of a great city full of artists and citizens who habitually did nothing'. Other citizens who habitually worked very hard indeed had much the same to say. In 1884, some 20 years after Mann's fictional heroine had so briefly played the rôle of Bavarian *Hausfrau*, the young Strauss wrote from Berlin to his childhood friend and fellow composer Ludwig Thuille, expressing his regrets that a tutorial post at Munich had prevented Thuille from coming with him, 'for the lethargic air of Munich is surely your artistic death.' Strauss was to return there for several seasons as conductor, but he always managed to steer clear of what he called 'Munich swamp fever'. He was fortunate: he took from the environment what was best about the Bavarian spirit – that genial humour with a sharp, satirical sting in the tail, later to be trumpeted in such liberal Munich papers as the celebrated *Simplicissimus*. His own infallible capacity for hard work, whatever the circumstances, was instilled by his father Franz, while his mother nurtured the tender side of his ardent spirit. Both were strengths of character which saw him unchanged and mostly unharmed through the greatest upheavals in European history.

By the time of Strauss's birth on 11 June 1864, the 18-year-old Ludwig II of Bavaria had been on the throne for three months, and shortly afterwards the patron king installed 'his' composer Richard Wagner in Munich. The complacency of the Munich burghers was shaken, and soon the conductor Hans von Bülow was putting the players of the Munich Court Orchestra through their paces for the first performances of *Tristan und Isolde* in 1864 and *Die Meistersinger* in 1868. (Ironically, Bülow's wife Cosima – the daughter of his friend Franz Liszt – was already in love with Wagner, and would eventually leave Bülow to marry him.) Bülow took over command of the Court Orchestra from the hard-working Franz Lachner in 1867, but his success was short-lived; like Wagner before him, he was well-nigh drummed out of town by the anti-Wagnerites.

Franz Strauss in his youth.

Leader of the opposition within the orchestra was its principal horn player, Franz Strauss. Haydn, Mozart and Beethoven were his gods, but for all his endless diatribes against 'that drunkard Wagner', he would go on to play the solos in *Tristan*, *Siegfried* and *Die Meistersinger* just as unforgettably as the ones in Beethoven's Ninth or the *Eroica*. His attitude to Bülow showed the same strict division between professional respect in the orchestra pit and hostile opposition outside it. Inflexible in the extreme, he remained obstinately seated when the rest of the players stood as a mark of respect for Wagner's death in 1883. But Franz Strauss's life had been a hard one. Richard later recorded in his reminiscences that his father had been orphaned and brought up by a stern uncle, but he didn't mention the additional fact that he lost his first wife and two children in a cholera epidemic. (In fact, Franz Strauss was 27 when his father died, but he had been sent away from his parents' home at an early age. Perhaps his reluctance to talk about the painful past led to error and omission on Richard's part.)

After a cautious seven-year courtship, Franz Strauss married for a second time in 1863. His new bride was Josepha Pschorr, daughter of a wealthy Munich brewery-owner Georg Pschorr. The newly-wedded couple lived in an apartment on the second floor of No. 2 Altheimereck, at the back of the brewery building, and it was here that Richard Georg was born, ten months later. In 1870, by which time the family had moved to a larger apartment in Sonnenstrasse, there followed a daughter, Johanna. It was a carefree childhood, Josepha doing her best to soothe her husband's phlegmatic temper.*

The Prussian struggle for supremacy and expansion remained in the background. Bavaria hardly felt the consequences of the campaign against Denmark to bring Schleswig-Holstein under German control in 1864. Nor was it affected by the privations of the Franco-Prussian War, which in 1870 brought the promise of a stable future – though like everywhere else in Germany, the south certainly reaped the benefits of the ensuing peace. Strauss grew up in an atmosphere of prosperity which increased in real terms as the century came to a close.

The family lived in a musical world-within-world, harbouring little concern for the political questions of the time. In later years, Josepha told her son that as a child he had been prompt to smile at the sound of the horn and cry with the violin. When he was four-and-a-half, he began piano lessons with August Tombo, harpist of

*The strain was eventually to tell on her delicate nerves; when Richard was in his mid-teens, his mother was admitted into psychiatric care, and spent periods of the rest of her life in institutions.

the Court Orchestra and a friend of his father. Tombo used to make him laugh by playing the middle notes of the piano with the tip of his nose. The orchestra's leader, Benno Walter, was a cousin of Franz, and must have been the tear-inducing violinist in question, for he was a regular visitor to Sonnenstrasse and taught the youngster to play the violin when he was seven. Strauss later depicted himself as a keen sight-reader but bad at practice. The child's talent for composition seems to have been more precocious: he wrote his *Schneiderpolka* (Tailor's Polka) at the age of six-and-a-half, with his father's assistance as scribe. Several other pieces, including songs for his aunt, received their premières at his uncle Georg's musical evenings. His initiation into the magic world of the opera came with visits to *Der Freischütz* and *Die Zauberflöte* at the Munich Court Opera in 1871; Johanna remembered that he took as much interest in the orchestra – Franz was playing, of course – as in the supernatural horrors of Weber's Wolf's Glen or in the antics of Papageno.

The two-year-old Richard.

One of the earliest photographs of Richard Strauss, aged one, with his mother, Josepha.

Richard Strauss, aged eight.

In 1875, after several years' elementary education at the Dom-Schule, Strauss went on to the Ludwigsgymnasium. His musical schooling continued with Hofkapellmeister Friedrich Meyer, who gave him a thorough grounding in theory, harmony and counterpoint, and he learned a great deal from watching and later playing first violin in his father's prestigious amateur orchestra, the *Wilde Gung'l*. According to his teachers, he was a boy of 'unclouded merriment and high spirits', unable to sit still for long and very bright in every subject except mathematics. The classical course which nurtured his love of the Greek world was fast becoming obsolete in the north of the country. Thomas Mann, once again in *Buddenbrooks*, recalls this old tradition – 'an end in itself, to be pursued at one's ease with a sense of joyous idealism' – as a great contrast to the 'state-within-state' policy of the joyless Prussian drilling under the banner of Kant, an education Strauss was lucky to avoid. Although he smarted under the burden of what he realised was unnecessarily dry and detailed grammatical study, he soon came to love the poetry and drama which this study allowed him to read. With the guidance of one of his classics masters, he set to music a section of a choral ode from Sophocles' *Electra*, and it was performed at an end-of-year concert in 1881. The piano reduction survives, and it shows us a simple, austere style in keeping with the current ideas about Greek calmness and grandeur fostered by Goethe and Winckelmann. Strauss was later to see for himself the vigour and violence in Greek art on his first trip to Greece, and his handling of the Electra myth was, he said, a violent reaction against the placid precepts of his education. He did not, however, forget those precepts, and in his old age he would pay as much of a tribute to the radiant purity of his early Hellenism in *Daphne* and *Die Liebe der Danae* as that offered, in his last instrumental works, to the musical example of his father.

Despite his son's obvious musical talent, Franz Strauss sensibly encouraged him to stay on at school for a further year – 'so that you will be able to take advantage of every opportunity'. In the winter of 1882-83, Strauss spent two terms at Munich University, and in spite of the tedium encountered during interminable lectures by dry-as-dust professors, he never lost a vital curiosity in his subjects – philosophy, aesthetics and history of art. All three proved vital in shaping his conception of the kind of music he wanted to compose. Inevitably, composition came first at that time, and his output during those apprentice years was enormous, much of it written in emulation of the approachable masters his father advised him to look at for example and instruction – among them Schumann, Mendelssohn and Spohr.

In 1881, Uncle Georg defrayed the costs of publishing the Festive March Strauss had written five years earlier (Franz conducted the first performance in a *Wilde Gung'l* concert). Breitkopf and Härtel were the somewhat unwilling recipients of this official Opus One, and it was Eugen Spitzweg, director of Joseph Aibl Verlag, who had enough faith in the young composer to publish more of his early works. Spitzweg's attempts to interest Hans von Bülow in the op.3 Piano Pieces of 1880-81 met with a characteristically blunt rejection: here was no genius, replied Bülow, but at best a talent. He had a chance to reform his opinion when he came across the Serenade in E flat for 13 wind

11

Brother and sister: Johanna
and Richard Strauss.

instruments written in November 1881, and he included it in the
repertory of the orchestra at Meiningen, where he was now court
conductor. Posterity has agreed with his judgement: a serene and
neatly-constructed work in which Strauss reached a sound
understanding of the medium he was writing for, the Serenade is
the earliest of his works to hold a place in the repertoire. Bülow's
esteem of the Serenade later brought forth another, more
substantial work for wind ensemble – the Suite for Woodwind –
though Bülow's pre-conceived scheme of movements gave Strauss
considerable difficulty.

   The teenager had become more adventurous in his experiments
with form and ensemble. He had moved on from piano works and

Franz Strauss in later life.

songs to short pieces for orchestra, a Piano Trio and a skilfully written String Quartet. All these compositions received royal treatment in the expert hands of Franz's colleagues, but the proudest moment for the father and son came in 1881, while Strauss was still in his final year at the Gymnasium: Hermann Levi and the Munich Court Orchestra gave the first performance of his Symphony in D minor. (Levi had taken command at the Munich Opera in 1872, and, a year after this lesser inauguration, he conducted the première of *Parsifal* at Bayreuth.) The critic of the *Münchner neueste Nachrichten* gave a fair assessment on 3 April:

The symphony . . . shows considerable competence in the treatment of the form as well as remarkable skill in orchestration. It must be said that the work cannot lay any claim to true originality, but it demonstrates throughout a fertile musical imagination, to which composition comes easily.

Auspicious performances of other works soon followed. On 5 December 1882, Strauss visited Vienna for the first time – 'just an ordinary city like Munich', he wrote home – accompanying Benno Walter in the violin and piano version of his Violin Concerto. The sparkling virtuoso writing for the soloist, particularly in the Mendelssohnian Finale, must have pleased Walter, and the début, Strauss told his parents, achieved a modest success: 'I, at least, didn't make a mess of the accompaniment', he added drily, though many rated his pianistic accomplishments rather more highly than he did. In Dresden, where he stayed before travelling to Berlin in the winter of 1883-84, he was delighted to make the acquaintance of Franz Wüllner. Wüllner had conducted the Dresden Court Orchestra in the first performance of the Wind Serenade the previous year, and, as principal conductor of the Cologne Gürzenich concerts, which he took over in 1884, was to become a champion of Strauss's tone-poems.

A winter in Berlin was the next stage in the educational policy unobtrusively planned by Franz Strauss for his son. After the gentle comforts of Munich, Berlin offered all the intoxications of a great city. Strauss learned to play skat (the card-game he pursued obsessively for the rest of his life), he danced the nights away at balls, flirted with his dancing-partners and absorbed the latest dramas with all the ardent passion of adolescence. Sardou's *Fedora* left him trembling for three hours, he wrote to Johanna, betraying modernist inclinations that his father would certainly have disdained. The playwright knew how 'to intensify conflict and passion to such a pitch that the audience almost loses its powers of sight and hearing.' He encountered for the first time the overtures of Berlioz, much preferring *Benvenuto Cellini* to *Le Carnaval Romain*, and he heard the works of Brahms. Franz

14

Johannes Brahms

disapproved, of course, but his son was not afraid to tell him about Brahms's Third Symphony, which he heard three times. After admitting initial incomprehension, he guardedly expressed his growing enthusiasm. To Ludwig Thuille he was less cautious: 'I'm beginning to get very attached to Brahms as a whole; he's always interesting and often very beautiful as well.' The Piano Quartet, which he completed in Berlin, was the first of his own works to show the influence – and to show it in abundance, though the drive and vigour were authentic enough.

He left Berlin on 29 March 1884, having completed, in addition to the Piano Quartet, a second Symphony (this time in F minor) and a Horn Concerto for his father. In Dresden he and Ferdinand Böckmann, principal cellist of the Court Orchestra, had given the first performance of the Cello Sonata, composed in 1882-83. Oscar Franz, Dresden's principal horn player, made some striking observations to his Munich counterpart, suggesting that the young Strauss was no Hamlet:

. . . it is indeed a splendid work, full of original feeling, and everything flows so wholesomely in it. Your son is fundamentally wholesome by nature, and I hope it will be many a long day before he is 'sicklied o'er with the pale cast of thought'.

Franz was right: however much more apparent the models may seem to us now, the rhythmic energy and vitality of the Sonata are unmistakable. So, too, is the arresting fanfare which opens the Horn Concerto, and the 'wholesomely flowing' *cantilenas* of its first two movements; still more remarkable, as a hint of things to come, the transformation of that rallying-cry into the high spirits of the Rondo. There are no hints of daring in the orchestration, for Strauss had not yet fallen under the spell of Wagner. He had seen *Siegfried, Die Walküre* and *Lohengrin* in his early teens, so he had not lacked opportunity, but at that point he saw no need to rebel against his father's attitude. Even his enthusiastic and revelatory study of the score of *Tristan* when he was 17 brought forth no results in his compositions, though that was surely the covert birth of his Wagnerian ambitions. It would take Bülow and his colleagues at Meiningen to bring them gradually to light. Yet the collision of interests was not to be a disastrous one: Strauss never did become a Hamlet, or even a pseudo-Hamlet, when the works abhorred by his father began to interest him. That 'wholesome' nature was to keep all the lessons and exercises of his classical education sensibly in mind.

Chapter 2

Court Conductor

Two meetings during that Berlin sojourn were shortly to bear fruit. While Bülow was rehearsing the Meiningen players in the Serenade, Strauss made the acquaintance of the orchestra's principal horn player Gustav Leinhos. Leinhos would be the soloist in the first performance of Strauss's Horn Concerto in April 1885, and now encouraged him in his dealings with the awesome Bülow. When Strauss met Bülow the great conductor spoke respectfully of his arch-enemy Franz. Yet despite this, and despite Bülow's undoubted admiration for his protegé's newly-commissioned Suite (which he furthermore entrusted to the young composer for his conducting début), there was certainly an opportunity for revenge – which was duly extracted when the occasion took place. Strauss was to conduct the Meiningen wind section in the Suite at a matinée concert in Munich's Odeonsaal on 18 November 1884. Bülow, he later recalled, was 'charmingly unbearable' about the way Munich had treated him in the Wagner débâcle, and seized his chance when the proud father came backstage to thank his son's benefactor:

'You have nothing to thank me for', he yelled. 'I haven't forgotten the way you treated me, here in this God-forsaken city. I did what I did today because your son has talent, not for your sweet sake.' Without another word my father left . . . all of a sudden Bülow was in the best of tempers . . .

Though this little melodrama soured the event for Strauss, it had been a successful début. He had been allowed no rehearsals, since Bülow told him his players could afford none on tour, and he could later remember nothing about the performance – conducting it, he confessed, in 'something of a haze'. Bülow must have been sufficiently impressed. The following May he announced he would be leaving Meiningen for engagements in Russia and elsewhere that winter; would Strauss take the chance of furthering his own conducting education in his absence? He needed a replacement, in any case, for his assistant Franz Mannstädt, who was taking a new position in Berlin. Strauss, 'at a loss for words', accepted without hesitation.

Hans von Bülow

The F minor Symphony was premièred in New York on 13 December 1884 under the baton of Theodor Thomas. The first European performance followed a month later in Cologne under Wüllner. Strauss had always found the developments forced upon him by sonata form problematic, and his second essay in full-scale symphonic thought suffered from similar shortcomings in this respect to its predecessor. He knew, all the same, that its almost calculated massiveness and grandeur were bold strokes owing little to Brahms; indeed, all but the Adagio had been completed before he arrived in Berlin and fell under Brahms's influence. 'Papa will open his eyes wide when he hears how modern the Symphony sounds', he gleefully wrote to his parents from Cologne, and the critics certainly opened their eyes in complimentary astonishment. It was his greatest musical success to date.

Shortly after Bülow's offer, the Duke of Meiningen confirmed

Meiningen in the mid-nineteenth century.

Strauss's appointment as court conductor. Among his disappointed rivals were Gustav Mahler, a passionate supporter of Bülow, and Felix Weingartner. The paths of Mahler, Weingartner and Strauss were to cross many times in the near future: Mahler and Strauss were to become friendly competitors as conductors and mutual helpmates as composers, accepting their differences (Mahler once said that they were tunnelling through different sides of the same mountain and would one day meet in the middle). The Meiningen position was a coveted one. The 48-strong orchestra had all the benefits of royal patronage and remained free from attachment to an opera company; it could rehearse repertoire with scrupulous thoroughness. The Viennese critic and anti-Wagnerite, Eduard Hanslick, praised Bülow's achievements. 'In precision the orchestra is surpassed and hardly has an equal', he wrote in 1884. 'Bülow conducts the orchestra as if it were a little bell in his hand.'

19

The Meiningen theatre company, too, established a legendary reputation, under the direction of the Duke, Georg II, who also designed the sets and costumes. The company travelled to London, Prague, Berlin and Moscow, where the Duke's concern for historical realism and ensemble acting captured the imagination of Stanislavsky and paved the way for his famous productions of Chekhov. Strauss was fortunate: the company stayed in Meiningen that winter of 1885-86, and he watched their performances of Shakespeare and Schiller spellbound, remembering in later years the wonderful handling of crowd scenes. When he came to leave, the Duke's morganatic wife, the actress Ellen Franz, remarked that they were losing the greatest cheerleader in the theatre.

Bülow remained in Meiningen during Strauss's first weeks, and the disciple eagerly watched him at work during rehearsals, absorbing everything. For his first concert on 25 October, he not only conducted his own F minor Symphony and the Suite for Woodwind, but also had Bülow's support while he took on the rôle of soloist in Mozart's C minor Piano Concerto, K.491. He was terrified of the part, and had rehearsed it for six months, but Bülow, writing to Spitzweg after rehearsals, judged 'his playing – like his conducting début – downright breathtaking' and wanted the publisher to print Strauss's cadenza (alas, no longer extant). Brahms, who was in Meiningen to hear Bülow give the first performance of his Fourth Symphony the day before this concert, drily judged Strauss's Symphony 'quite charming', and added some advice which the acolyte never forgot: that he should 'take a look at Schubert's dances and practise inventing simple eight-bar melodies.' He also criticised 'thematic trifling', and Strauss, recalling the incident, remarked that his later concentration on counterpoint only when it sprang from poetic necessity was a result of this observation. Needless to say, his father was pleased with the verdict, using it to insist, as he did at every available opportunity in his letters, on the virtues of clarity and simplicity.

The schedule of performances and rehearsals – the rehearsals starting at 10am and running for anything up to five hours – exhausted Strauss, more because of the energy he put in than the time involved (though as he later remarked, 'those were the days when the eight hour working day was unheard of'). He also had charge of the chamber concerts and the choral society. His conducting, executed with wild, sweeping gestures, bespoke his youthful enthusiasm, though Bülow found it helpfully elastic. Franz, hearing a colourful report, wrote upbraiding 'serpentine gestures in a beanpole like you'. Those who recall the composer conducting in later years, minimal in his movements but capable of exacting the subtlest *rubato* from the players he disciplined so thoroughly, might well wonder at the steady process and effort of will by which he had learned to master his earlier impetuosity.

One morning at an orchestral rehearsal during his first few weeks in Meiningen, the Duke's wife asked to hear Wagner's *Der Fliegende Holländer* overture, 'and I, with unexampled impudence, never having set eyes on the score before, conducted a brisk and breezy performance of it at sight; it went very well', he wrote to Hermann Levi. Bülow's enthusiasm for the music of Wagner had cooled after Cosima had left him, but Strauss's Wagnerian discipleship was now ripening. As the older conductor joined the ranks of the Brahmsians, now established in opposition to the iconoclastic school of Wagner, his pupil, who had made a logical progression from Franz Strauss's pantheon of immortals to Brahms, approached the *Zukunftsmusik* (the music of the future). This was embodied in the works of Wagner, Liszt and Berlioz – then considered the leaders of the *avant-garde*.

Alexander Ritter, a composer who happened also to be a violinist in the Meiningen Orchestra, was an avid supporter of the new trends, and it was he who encouraged Strauss to follow them in his own music. Richly articulate and a keen debater, Ritter outlined to him the decline of Beethoven's expressive force in what he characterised as the rambling structures of Bruckner and the empty vessels of Brahms, and its salvation in the symphonic poem through the strength of a governing idea or 'programme' – as exemplified in the orchestral works of Liszt. (Liszt was an important influence on Wagner in this regard, as were the writings of the philosopher Schopenhauer. Programmes were nearly as old as music itself; it was the operation of the idea which really covered new ground. For Liszt and Wagner it was a crucial justification for experiments in harmony so far unheard of in music.) Strauss was to describe Ritter as 'the man to whom I owe more than to any other human being, living or dead. Ritter's advice marked the turning point in my career.'

So, too, in happy conjunction, did the holiday Strauss took between contracts. Bülow had resigned his position in December 1885, as he had planned, and in January Strauss, who was acting as the interim conductor, heard that the Duke intended to reduce the orchestra to 39 players. By chance, he had just received an offer from Carl Perfall, Intendant of the Munich Court Orchestra, to take up the position of third conductor there the following season, and on 1 February 1886 he accepted. At his last Meiningen concert, his programme consisted of Brahms's Fourth Symphony and St Antony Variations, songs by Wagner, and the Prelude and *Liebestod* from *Tristan*.

He had composed very little during this busy time – only a Scherzo for piano and orchestra which Bülow dismissed as

Alexander Ritter

Rome – omnibus bound for
St Peter's, late 1880s.

unplayable (later to resurface as the *Burleske*) – but the necessary
'ideas' preached by Ritter materialised obligingly on his Italian
holiday that spring. The equable traveller, undaunted by the theft
of his suitcase, responded typically with exuberant mirth rather
than romantic awe when he saw Vesuvius erupting, though the
humanity of Raphael stirred him to the depths of his soul;
Michelangelo's glories he found admirable but somehow less
approachable. 'In the ruins of Rome', he reported to Bülow, 'I
discovered that ideas just come simply, in flocks.' The Forum
spirits eventually found a place in the second movement of his
'symphonic fantasia' *Aus Italien* which he sketched in the south
and scored in Munich, completing it on 22 September. At the time
of the work's première in 1887, he laid out in a letter to the
musicologist Karl Wolff a manifesto which was to hold good for
every one of his experiments in the new Ritter-prompted genre:

. . . external features [are] of purely secondary importance . . . it
consists of *sensations evoked by* the sight of the wonderful natural beauties
of Rome and Naples, not *descriptions* of them . . . *Expression* is our art,
and a piece of music which has nothing truly poetic to convey to me –
content, that is, of course, which can be properly represented *only in
music*, a content that words may be able to *suggest but only suggest* – a piece
like that in my view is anything you care to call it, but not music.

23

Aus Italien sets the old and new influences side by side; its finest passages are totally characteristic of the mature composer. The second movement, 'Ruins of Rome', still shows very clear traces of Mendelssohn, Schumann and above all Brahms, and illustrates the kind of problems Strauss was encountering with the conventions of sonata form. But the movements encircling it breathe the new-found freedom springing from the emancipation of form. The magical, Lisztian harmonies of the prospect over a misty-morning Campagna, the sudden emergence of a fresh melody mid-way through the same movement and the way the strings extemporise in its wake, the free flow of the Sorrento Andante which Debussy especially admired when he heard it: all of these seem to be linked to the spontaneous process of ideas. Here, too, the soft light and blue skies of the south appear to have seeped into the orchestration, the colour and warmth of which had not been foreshadowed in any of Strauss's previous works. In the Finale, he embroidered a song he had heard in the streets of Naples with a riot of high-spirited bustle, and crowned it with a helter-skelter coda. The fact that the tune was no folk-song but Denza's ever-popular 'Funiculi, funicula' – Strauss would jest that one could tell he had been in Naples after the plague! – made no difference: the more the rebel could raise his listeners' eyebrows the better.

The players at the first Berlin performance in 1888 (Strauss's conducting début with the Berlin Philharmonic) certainly caught his infectious high spirits: 'these people have such expression . . .' he wrote to his father, 'a freshness, a youthful ardour, and they played the fantasy with great enthusiasm and love . . . The first time they read through the Finale the orchestra burst out laughing, people have such a sense of humour here.' Bülow felt that Strauss had gone almost too far in his demands; if anything, the ideas were too prodigious. But he was right in describing this as a 'wonderful mistake'. In the works that followed, Strauss would learn how to shuffle the conventions of the old forms with the shock of the new as a skilled practitioner of his trade.

Chapter 3

A Wagnerian in Weimar

Hermann Levi gave his third conductor at the Munich Court Opera repertoire that proved, on the whole, less than rewarding. The occasional masterpiece came Strauss's way: the second opera he conducted was Mozart's *Così fan tutte*, then placed rather low in the Mozart canon – and indeed it was Strauss who was later instrumental in restoring it to its rightful place in public esteem. He also had his chances with Verdi's *Il trovatore* and *Un ballo in maschera*, which gave him the opportunity to revise his low opinion of Italian opera manifest in the letters of his recent holiday (*Falstaff* had been a notable exception, and was to remain his favourite Verdi opera). More often he was entrusted with the operas of Lortzing, Auber, Flotow, Rheinberger and Nicolai. He recalled in his reminiscences that he lacked the 'routine' necessary for so much hack-work; adept as he was at taking command, he often went about his preparation in a cavalier and condescending fashion, and his 'idiosyncratic insistence on "my own tempos"' predictably alarmed both his father, still the orchestra's principal horn, and, more seriously, Intendant Perfall, who lodged several complaints about this unruly habit. The crowning disappointment for the third-in-command was to be given the rehearsals for the première, nearly 55 years after it had been written, of Wagner's first opera *Die Feen*, only to have the performance itself snatched away from him on the grounds that it could not be entrusted to a mere Musikdirektor.

On a more positive note, those three seasons at Munich, from 1886 to 1889, were enlivened by several invitations to conduct his F minor Symphony in other cities: in 1887 he travelled to Frankfurt, Milan and Leipzig, where he met Gustav Mahler, praising his skill in tempo modification to Bülow. And by dint of its very dullness, the stolid fare of his Munich diet served to fire his compositional enthusiasm. A Violin Sonata from the later part of 1887 is impressively big-boned, straining to break the limits of its form. But this was to be his farewell chamber music; Ritter, back in Munich by a happy coincidence, was a constant presence urging him back to the symphonic poem. They met nearly every evening at a Munich wine parlour, the older man encouraging the younger in his reading of Schopenhauer. The combination of the philosopher with the other authors Strauss was excitedly reading at the time – Dostoyevsky, Tolstoy and Ibsen – led the young composer away from the Italian sunlight towards a darker, more dramatic literary world. His imagination was caught by the subject of Macbeth, whose story was to give him all the opportunity he needed for dark colours and dissonance; it would be 'very wild in character', he announced as he worked on it after the Munich triumph of *Aus Italien* in March 1887.

At the beginning of 1888, he sent the draft score of *Macbeth* to Bülow, who overcame his aversion to this densely-wrought, designed-to-shock music of the future and made several helpful suggestions. He was right to point out that a work dealing with the ambition and guilt of the protagonist and his wife should not end with the victory march of Malcolm and Macduff, mere *comprimarii*: was that not, after all, exactly the kind of self-consciously 'literary' music the new tone poet had sought to avoid? So Strauss changed the ending, but although rehearsals took place at Mannheim and Meiningen, *Macbeth* had to wait until 1890 for its first performance in Weimar. By this time, Strauss had the experience of two more tone poems – *Don Juan* and *Tod und Verklärung* – behind him, and felt the earlier work to be overscored. Accordingly, he revised the orchestration – though not as much, needless to say, as his father would have liked (Franz wrote a typically admonitory letter to his son after the Weimar performance, reminding him as usual that 'great and noble ideas' should be simply attired). When this final version was heard in Berlin in 1892 he was well satisfied. 'The orchestra played wonderfully, the piece sounded fabulous and . . . with the clarity of the new version . . . there isn't a single theme that doesn't "stand out".' There were still problems – particularly that of the music being led, in Lisztian fashion, by the story line, at the expense of structural coherence and concentration of expression. On the other hand, the striking Wagnerian colours of two tenor trombones, bass trumpet, bass trombone, tenor tuba, bass clarinet and contrabassoon extended the symphonic poem's means of creating the necessary atmosphere. By 1891, Strauss had learned more about orchestration.

The first sketches for *Don Juan* were made on a second visit to Italy in the early summer of 1888, in the cloisters of a church in Padua. On his return, Strauss began to compose. This time, the 'programme' owed rather less to literary treatments of the legend (including Nikolaus Lenau's unfinished verse-drama quoted as preface to the score) than to the purpose the Don Juan legend served for articulating the composer's own experience.

On holiday at his relatives' villa in Feldafing the previous summer, he had been introduced to the de Ahna family and had agreed to give singing lessons to Major-General de Ahna's eldest daughter, Pauline. She had studied singing at the Munich Conservatory, and Strauss, captivated as much by her musical accomplishment as by her personal charms, wrote to her former teacher, Max Steinitzer, enthusing: 'She is much more talented than you think; we have only to bring her gifts out.'

At this time there hung a question-mark over Strauss's attachment to Dora, wife of the Munich Court Orchestra's principal cellist, Hanus Wihan (the dedicatee of the op.6 Cello Sonata and later to be similarly honoured by Dvořák when he wrote his Cello Concerto in 1895). In 1886, Franz had been worrying about gossip concerning the time his son spent with Dora and the few remaining letters from the correspondence between Strauss and Dora point to an intimate friendship. The last from Dora, in 1893, subtly hints at a poignant remembrance of things past. But by then, Pauline was in the ascendant. Strauss moved to Weimar in October 1889 to take up the post of Conductor at the Court Theatre, and Pauline arrived shortly after. From then on, the environment in which they shared rehearsals and performances of songs and operas allowed plenty of time for a love affair to flourish.

Strauss, jaded by his experiences in Munich, had taken some time to consider the offer of the Weimar post from the Intendant, Hans von Bronsart. Although his demand for the influential position of Hofkapellmeister was denied him, and the salary was less than he earned in Munich, he had to consider that his artistic freedom would be more considerable. He was also convinced that Weimar, where Liszt had established a stronghold both for his own works and those of Berlioz and Wagner during his ten-year tenure there, would be no less responsive to his own Wagnerian wishes. In this he was not disappointed.

He had already established close links with Bayreuth in the summer of 1889, before taking up his position at Weimar. Bülow, who had kindled Bronsart's interest in the young conductor, had also recommended him as musical assistant at Wagner's festival theatre – realising no doubt that he would be pushing his pupil further in the direction from which he himself was increasingly retreating. Strauss found the work demanding, but less exhausting than leaping from one repertory opera to another in a different style because 'it's the mixture of different things that one usually has to gobble down which is so dreadfully tiring'. Working on the production of *Parsifal*, he began his long association with Cosima Wagner and earned her immediate approval when he told her that he had replaced Brahms's *German Requiem* with Liszt's *Héroïde funèbre* on a Wiesbaden engagement.

The court theatre at Weimar.

Arriving in Weimar on 8 September, Strauss found that the ageing Eduard Lassen, conductor-in-chief, was not prepared to relinquish his *Meistersinger, Holländer* and *Ring* to the 25-year-old he regarded as a genius. Yet when Strauss heard that he was to conduct *Lohengrin*, scheduled for the first few weeks of October, he lavished all his energies on the production. This he reported as successful, though he lamented the way in which the singers fell back on routine gestures. Not until the 100th performance of *Lohengrin* in Weimar in 1891 was Strauss able to ensure that the occasion received its due, by taking part in every aspect of the production, which included the choice of new scenery and costumes, and earning Cosima's deepest gratitude.

Ever since he had studied the score as a teenager, however, it was *Tristan und Isolde* which remained Strauss's conducting ambition. Convalescing from a bout of pneumonia in 1891, he told Ritter that his thoughts 'performed half acts of *Tristan* from memory', and although he was not strong enough to conduct *Tannhäuser* and *Parsifal* at Bayreuth that summer, ample compensation came in using the time to prepare for a Weimar

Cosima with Richard Wagner.

Tristan. It was to be a landmark in setting new standards for Wagner performances: the opera was to be given absolutely complete (invariably, it had been performed with substantial cuts) and meticulously rescored to suit the size of the Weimar orchestra, partly to satisfy Cosima's zealous concern that every word should be heard (an invaluable exercise to be remembered when Strauss made his own essays in operatic form). In addition, as he wrote to Cosima, the revision had its own distinctive merits: 'the orchestral writing has acquired something intimate, like chamber music, and the absence of the score's attractions gives it a unique attraction'. The first night, on 17 January 1892, was a great success due largely to Pauline's youthful, charming Isolde and the merits of another pupil of Strauss's, the tenor Hans Zeller, as Tristan. The conductor waxed lyrical to Cosima over the

Cosima in old age, the
'Mistress of Bayreuth'.

Richard Strauss as a young
conductor at Weimar. These
photos were sent, with
affectionate captions, to
his fellow-composer,
Humperdinck.

elasticity of the orchestral response, adding 'now I've conducted *Tristan* for the first time, and it was the most wonderful day of my life.'

Cosima, who had set strict observances over the necessity for slow tempi in her late husband's music, showed a surprising enthusiasm for Strauss's flexible, impulsive view of *Tristan*. One critic who watched Strauss conducting the Prelude noted how his 'drawing in and letting out of a single breath' owed a great deal to the Bülow tradition. But this was not enough to shield him from Intendant Bronsart's growing disapproval, expressed in the early Weimar days in the form of fatherly advice, over his fast speeds and impetuous temperament (there were harsh words, too, for the interference of 'Wagner's unmusical widow'). For some time Strauss's relations with Bronsart remained uneasy, though he later admitted that his obstinate behaviour 'squandered good will' unnecessarily.

Meanwhile, *Don Juan* had its first performance in Weimar on 11 November 1889. Strauss had wanted a première elsewhere, because of the restricted number of Weimar strings, but in the event he was more than satisfied with the results: 'the sound was wonderful, with an immense glow and sumptuousness', he wrote to his father after rehearsals. At the concert the horn players

sweated and cursed but the audience cheered loudly. Inevitably the breathtaking brilliance of the orchestration led the conservatives to suspect the absence of purely musical ideas. Franz's plea for 'less outward glitter and more content' was echoed by the critic Eduard Hanslick when he heard the tone-poem the following year:

In the one-sided study of these three orchestral geniuses [Liszt, Wagner and Berlioz] the younger generation has developed a virtuosity in the creation of sound effects beyond which it is not possible to go. Colour is everything, musical thought nothing.

Accusations of this kind worried Strauss. As conductor, his remedy was to stress the sweep and verve of the work (cast, like *Macbeth*, in sonata-form with two episodes, but more tautly

Eduard Hanslick

32

constructed) which he felt Bülow, among others, missed at a slower speed. As for the 'sound effects', it appears even more obvious today that a clutch of striking thematic ideas have found their expression on instruments supremely apt to their characters: it is hard to think of an orchestral solo more suited to the oboe than the plaintive episode evocatively coloured by lowered strings and muted horns (Strauss was justly proud of this), or writing for unison horns more thrilling than the octave cry which takes us unawares immediately afterwards. This was one daring departure from tradition; another was the final plunge into darkness after so much hectic brilliance – a masterstroke to crown Strauss's first masterpiece.

Work on the next tone-poem, *Tod und Verklärung* (Death and Transfiguration), had begun at Easter 1889, while Strauss was still in Munich, and the score was ready soon after the first performance of *Don Juan*. Apart from the *Macbeth* revision, with which its sombre orchestration in some passages has much in common, it was the only substantial fruit of those first three years at Weimar. The 'programme', with its graphic depiction of a dying man's agonised review of his life and the transfigured aftermath, had at that time no personal associations for Strauss. He would only say that the ways of artistic inspiration were strange indeed; perhaps, as he pointed out on several occasions, it was a need to ring the changes on *Don Juan* by progressing from the protagonist's C minor anguish to the resolution beyond death of his earthly ideals in C major – exactly the opposite of Juan's haunting fate. Contrast, the need to move on to something new and breathe a different world into each fresh work, became increasingly important to Strauss. But whatever his real motives for turning to this theme, he would be able to say on his death-bed that dying was just as he had composed it here. He had great affection for the theme which embodied the hero's 'ideology', stated in full at the heart of the work, quoting it three more times in the course of his lifetime. Its serene apotheosis in the final section has been much maligned for its failure to touch the sublime, but in sympathetic hands it glows as his later attempts at a similar resolution (in *Die Frau ohne Schatten* and *Friedenstag*) never can.

The first performance of *Tod und Verklärung* took place in Eisenach on 21 June 1890, with Strauss again conducting, in a concert that included the *Burleske*, a scherzo for piano and orchestra, composed at Meiningen. (Mercurial and playful in mood, it made an ideal contrast to the tone-poem, even though its rather heavy-handed sonata form structure was clearly influenced by Brahms.) Cosima for once found herself in agreement with Hanslick: she thought the tone-poem arid and dogged by technique, a further step along the primrose path from *Don Juan*, which she had found similarly dominated by intellect. It may have been her influence that prevented Strauss from writing another orchestral work during the next five years and turned him towards his first operatic emulation of the Bayreuth master. He could hardly have chosen a more Wagnerian theme for it than that of the secret religious orders of the Middle Ages who wandered the land making stands against the profanities of the Minnesingers. His research on the subject was thorough and informed with his readings of Schopenhauer. He proceeded with his own libretto, completing it in the autumn of 1890. In March of 1892 he completed the Prelude, sure that its simplicity, so obviously echoing *Lohengrin* (one of a handful of Wagner's early operas which Franz could tolerate), would please both his father and the Wagnerians. But the crucial work on this new opera, *Guntram*, was to come in a different climate.

That same year, 1892, relations with Bayreuth became strained. Pauline, who had sung Elisabeth in *Tannhäuser* and a Flower-Maiden in *Parsifal* the previous summer, was not invited back; nor was Zeller. Strauss was offered rehearsals and the last two performances only of *Meistersinger* (the rest were to go to Hans Richter). At first, conscious of the Munich quarrel over *Die Feen*, he complained to Cosima that he was no 'plodding rehearsal taker' and with her peacemaking promise of *Tristan* as a conducting bonus for him, matters for the moment reached a halt. There was trouble, too, with Bronsart and Lassen and a cooling of the friendship with Bülow. Then illness struck for the second time, with redoubled severity, and Uncle Georg Pschorr, at whose home Strauss had convalesced less than a year earlier, again played the benevolent godfather. The ideal cure, he thought, for his nephew's pleurisy and bronchitis would be a long holiday in Greece and Egypt, and he offered him a present of money which would make it possible. This was the perfect answer to the problems Strauss had incurred as a result of his highly-strung temperament: an opportunity, as he explained to Cosima, to take stock in isolation.

Rarely did Strauss give a more searching insight into his behaviour than in an assessment of the situation to his friend Eugen Lindner while convalescing:

I really believed that I had always applied my ethical principles in practice to the best of my abilities. You should not forget, my dear Lindner, that this honest application often meets with the most remarkable obstacles, even in my own breast, which put all my good intentions at risk and, with the help of my distinctly overwrought nerves, often encourages the most extraordinary blossoming of paradox or, if you want it in plain language, nonsense. One of these obstacles is *a devil of opposition*, who means well but who has three powerful enemies in the world, and he goes crazy at the sight of them; those three enemies are hypocrisy, the impudence of dilettantes and philistinism . . . However, I really must put up a serious defence of myself against the charge of intolerance; I do not believe that there are many people who make a more honest and sincere attempt to do justice to everything that is beautiful, or at least *is produced by serious artistic endeavour*, and to *exercise and express* that judgment as long as I find myself in the company of *honest, truthful* artistic understanding . . .

Time and change of place were all he needed now, and his travels would offer them in abundance. If they produced other results which were to shock his mentors, then they too would be the result of a sincere resolution to follow his own path. He left for Greece on 4 November 1892, taking with him the libretto, and the first two acts in short score, of *Guntram*.

Chapter 4

Striking a Path

'From the moment when, coming from Brindisi, I saw from the deck of the Italian steamer the island of Corfu and the blue mountains of Albania, I have always been a German Greek, even to this day', Strauss recalled in his old age. His travels took him to Olympia, where for the first time we find him struggling to express in words his feelings on the sublime, and where the violent scenes on the friezes of Zeus's temple told him that Greek art was not all calmness and austerity. He proceeded to Athens and was moved to tears by the beauty of the Parthenon. In a letter to Cosima he was following Ruskin's observations after his own fashion, reflecting on a time when architecture, art, religion and race had all been one; Bayreuth, by way of contrast with the Greek world, represented 'the utmost isolation of the Christian genius', passing above the heads of a largely unheeding people. By the time of that communication it was early December and he had arrived in Cairo. Egyptian temples, he confided to Ritter from his journey down the Nile, stood in relation to their Greek counterparts as Bach's B minor Mass did to Mozart's G minor (40th) Symphony – imposing, but lacking in human grace. He felt a bracing freedom from routine, and told another colleague that he could happily settle in the Egyptian desert writing opera upon opera. After the storm and stress of his Munich and Weimar years he was in no doubt that this was the change he had long required.

He completed *Guntram* in Cairo on Christmas Eve, adding at the foot of the short score '*Deo gratia* (and St Wagner)'. In fact he had now decided upon an ending which he knew would displease the sacristans of Bayreuth. Until then, the plot had been undiluted, convoluted Wagner; but now that Guntram was due to atone for the murder of his beloved Freihild's despotic husband, Strauss decided that he should reject the expiation prescribed by Guntram's mentor from the sacred brotherhood and announce that he himself would decide his fate. Freihild's assumption that the power of love had triumphed would prove equally incorrect; Guntram was to leave her solemnly, taking his penance upon himself. Ritter, who had eagerly followed the opera's progress, was horrified when his disciple wrote and told him what he now intended. On 17 January 1893 Strauss received his reply, which described the news as 'one of the most profoundly painful things I have ever experienced' and commended Schopenhauer, the Gospels and Wagner's *Art and Religion* as correctives. Strauss asserted in turn that he kept only the best of literary company, but that in any case personal experience must come first, and he had expressed something which he happened to feel strongly.

Essentially the end of *Guntram* was his first attempt to express a personal philosophy steering a positive middle ground between the element in Schopenhauer that Wagner only eventually came to express – the negation of the will (it was this which Ritter believed he was bound to uphold) – and Nietzsche's and Stirner's emphasis on egotism as all-powerful. His 'philosophy', in fact, was little more than an expression of his own individuality, a need to be free from any single creed and to follow Goethe's advice that one should 'find nothing uninteresting or not worth the trouble of looking at closely'. For some critics Strauss's work exists in a moral or intellectual vacuum – it bears Hanslick's label of 'pleasure gas'; for many others its very strength lies in its variousness. This new

Sphinx and pyramids, Gizeh, circa 1900.

Strauss with fellow-travellers, Aswan.

Strauss in the year of his marriage, 1894.

freedom came from the time his Egyptian winter gave him to assimilate his reading and experience. As he told Josef Gregor in 1945, 'my path was clear at last for uninhibitedly independent creation'.

In retrospect it seems ironic that the home-grown ethics Ritter and the Bayreuth school found so objectionable came, for the most part, enveloped in Wagnerian chain mail, though Guntram's first act monologue and his final scene with Freihild in the crucial third act point distinctively to a new vein of warm, euphonious rhapsodising. Brushed aside as it is by a cumbersome Wagnerian manner for Guntram's religious aspirations, the hero's apostrophe to nature finds Strauss revelling in soaring writing for strings and woodwind birdsong, and it strikes as rather more than 'the shiny veneer of dark illusion' that Guntram calls it. Once his mind is finally made up, this flowing style re-establishes itself in an epilogue of serene assurance, the first of many in Strauss's music. He wrote of this last act that it was 'hyper *Tristan*ish . . . [but] the most advanced in the precision of expression, the richest and most impressive in the melodic invention, and altogether by far the best thing I've ever written'.

Strauss continued the orchestration of *Guntram* in Sicily during the spring. Back in Germany, the gloom of being back on the Weimar treadmill was lightened by hopes for the opera's first performance. Munich had been his choice, but it was in Weimar that *Guntram* saw the light of day in May 1894. Strauss became 'conductor, repetiteur, set-painter, stage manager and theatrical costumier' rolled into one, he told Ritter, with whom he was still on speaking terms. The large orchestra he wanted had to be reduced, given the restricted number of Weimar strings; for the triple woodwind, extra players were recruited from the local military band. The press was generally indifferent, though a first review in the *Münchner neueste Nachrichten* judged *Guntram* to be individual and musically free of Wagnerian taint, and in a detailed article Max Hasse considered that the music transfigured the final scene so far as to dissolve all qualms about the actual idea behind it. Strauss's two pupils took the principal rôles. Poor Zeller, not surprisingly, was worn out by the insanely taxing title part (160 bars longer than the rôle of Tristan) but Pauline shone as Freihild. Two days later, on 12 May, her engagement to Strauss was officially announced.

In fact the engagement had secretly taken place back in March, when Pauline's father, Major-General de Ahna, had granted the promising young musican's request for his daughter's hand. Moody and insecure, Pauline would in later years baffle acquaintances with her tantrums and her acid remarks; to them there was little evidence of the deep love and affection underpinning this 'perfect' marriage. One of her favourite pronouncements was that her parents had held grave misgivings about the suitability of the match; the real circumstances were quite different, and tell us a great deal about the foundations of the relationship. A touching letter from Pauline to Strauss on 24 March 1894 makes clear that she herself was the one to hold reservations, and not because she thought a mere composer beneath a general's daughter:

. . . You should not overestimate me, and your parents and Hanna know my moods too; O God, and now I am suddenly supposed to turn in to a model housewife, so that you do not feel disappointed. Dear friend, I am afraid that it will fail, and the more everyone else rejoices the more oppressed I feel . . . forgive this letter but the two feelings – my happiness and my fear of a new life – weigh on me so that I am only half capable of reasoning.

About the future of her own singing career she need not have worried. Strauss gave her every opportunity to carry on and it was only her wish to become a mother that put an end to her public engagements. Her father warned her that to turn back now would

Wedding ensemble,
10 September 1894,
Marquartstein.

create enormous difficulties, praising his future son-in-law in generous terms, and her sister advised her to 'be a little "incarnate poetry" (as Count Wedell called your Isolde) offstage as well'.

Several accounts have been given concerning the manner of the official engagement in Weimar; that narrated by Strauss to Lotte Lehmann remains the most entertaining. According to the great soprano, Strauss and Pauline argued over some interpretative point during a rehearsal (presumably of *Guntram* and not *Tannhäuser*, as her story has it) and the quarrel culminated in Pauline hurling the score at Strauss's head and storming off to the dressing room. Strauss followed. Members of the orchestra stood fearfully outside the door listening to the uproar within. A delegation approached.

Strauss opened the door and stood in the doorway beaming radiantly. The representative of the orchestra stammered his speech: 'The orchestra is so horrified by the incredibly shocking behaviour of Fräulein Pauline de Ahna, that they feel they owe it to their honoured conductor to refuse in the future to play in any opera in which she might have a part . . .' Strauss regarded the musicians smilingly. 'That hurts me very much, for I have just become engaged to Fräulein de Ahna.'

The wedding took place in Marquartstein on 10 September 1894, a month after Pauline had sung Elisabeth for a second time at Bayreuth, with Strauss still sufficiently in the graces of Cosima to conduct this *Tannhäuser*. As a wedding present, Strauss presented Pauline with four songs (op.27) which remain among the most popular of his enormous output in this field: 'Ruhe, meine Seele!',

41

Pauline Strauss with the one-year-old Franz, 1898.

'Cäcilie', 'Heimliche Aufforderung' and 'Morgen!'. (The latter two songs used some of the more conventional love-lyrics by the Scotts-born anarchist John Henry Mackay.) Up until the turn of the century – and these were the years most prolific in songs – Strauss would extend his range of subjects to include settings of the *Jugendstil* or 'new age' poets, reflecting the social concerns of Richard Dehmel's *Der Arbeitsmann* (The Worker) and Karl Henckell's *Lied des Steinklopfers* (Song of the Stonecutter). These lyrical tributes to Pauline, together with the fervent masterpieces that make up his op.10, written at the age of 18 (including 'Zueignung', 'Die Nacht' and 'Allerseelen', most probably inspired by his love-affair with Dora Wihan), are the songs of Strauss we hear most often today.

On several occasions Pauline would appear as soloist in her husband's songs, and a great number of them were written with her voice in mind. She had a considerable reputation as a *Lieder* singer as well as for her stage rôles; even Hanslick condescended to call her the composer's 'better and more beautiful other half'. Strauss invariably accompanied her and praised her exemplary breath control, particularly in the long phrases of Pamina's aria from Mozart's *Die Zauberflöte*, Elisabeth's prayer and his own 'Traum durch die Dämmerung', 'Morgen!' and 'Freundliche Vision'. Freihild was the only one of his operatic characters she ever portrayed on stage, but a whole host of other unforgettable female characters throughout the operas to come would owe their 'life' to her. Pauline's too is the credit for the understanding Strauss shows for the soprano voice, reflected in the rewarding, sympathetic lines he wrote for it. There again, only the finest technique is good enough.

There was cause for mourning as well as celebration in 1894. Hans von Bülow had died in Cairo on 12 February. Strauss refused to conduct a memorial concert in Hamburg towards the end of the month unless he could dictate a programme consisting of Wagner and Liszt as well as Beethoven; and when he did take over Bülow's Berlin Philharmonic concerts, it was only for one season – his contract was not renewed and Artur Nikisch superseded him in 1895.

1894 was also Strauss's last year at Weimar and during it he added to the distinction of the *Guntram* première the first performance of Humperdinck's *Hänsel und Gretel*, a work for which he always retained a special admiration. In October new overtures from Levi, which had begun while he was still on his travels, brought him back to Munich. Terms on this occasion gave him the post of associate conductor and, as a result, the coveted title of *Hofkapellmeister* – on condition that he behaved himself. This time he conducted *Die Meistersinger* and *Tristan* when Levi fell ill and had more scope for introducing 'new' works, among them Liszt's *Faust Symphony*, which one reactionary Munich paper described as displaying 'the newest trends in music' forty years after it had been composed.

At its Munich première on 16 November 1895 *Guntram* was conclusively felled by the conservatives and the Wagnerians alike. After this one performance, and a few isolated revivals during the first decade of the twentieth century, no more was heard of it until 1934 when Strauss, who had affectionately set up a gravestone for his 'honourable and virtuous youth' in the grounds of his Garmisch villa, resuscitated the 'corpse' by reorchestrating it and making several substantial and selective cuts.

Chapter 5

The Organised Romantic

Mozart was one composer who gained from Strauss's increased control over operatic repertoire during his second term at Munich. There was a new production of *Don Giovanni* at the Residenztheater in May 1896, joined the following year by *Così fan tutte* and *Die Entführung aus dem Serail*. Strauss, who now received much credit for his meticulous rehearsing of this then-unfamiliar repertoire and for his elaborate improvisations in the *secco* recitatives, became one of the first interpreters to militate against the concept of Mozart as nothing more than a playful and elegant child of the Rococo age. In 1944 he summed up his attitude:

. . . his work, although it is transfigured, ethereal and far from harsh reality, embraces the entire range of human emotions, from the monumental and gloomy grandeur of the supper scene in *Don Giovanni* to the delicacy of Zerlina's arias, the heavenly frivolity of *Figaro* and the detached irony of *Così fan tutte* . . . it is senseless as well as superficial to postulate a uniform Mozartian style for the performances of these infinitely delicate and highly articulate psychological studies.

Such observations may seem obvious to us now; they were by no means so at the turn of the century. The discovery and detailed understanding of Mozart's operas was to have a vital effect on Strauss's later compositions, and when he came to leave Munich for the second time in 1898, the number of his Mozart performances had outnumbered those of Wagner operas.

This was not, however, any indication of a declining interest in Wagner's works. But by now he had freed himself from the rule of Cosima and Ritter and had celebrated that freedom with the first of the tone-poems to owe nothing stylistically to Liszt, Wagner or Berlioz – *Till Eulenspiegel* (op.28). Once again, the battle against Munich lethargy had produced a fresh flourish of compositions. The germ of a *Don Juan* opera, considered after the success of the tone-poem, suggests that Strauss had been striving for a new form with human characters. Exactly the opposite happened with the legend of Till Eulenspiegel, which Strauss had drafted as the plot of an opera back in Weimar in the autumn and winter of 1894.

The National Theatre, Munich, in the 1890s.

Till, the eternal mischief-maker and outsider, became a Nietzschean figure responding with savage criticism to the philistine burghers of Schilda, his extreme behaviour set alongside the golden mean of a loving couple. The project became increasingly enmeshed in dense philosophising and reached a halt with the failure of *Guntram*, which inevitably put a stop to any more operatics for the time being.

Instead Strauss remoulded the essence of Till's character closer to Carl Simrock's version of the old German folk-tale and turned his work into an orchestral study. About its origins we know little, save for a note to Wüllner on 9 June 1895 telling him that the work was completed and that it had turned out to be 'very funny and high-spirited'. Wüllner gave the first performance with his Cologne orchestra on 5 November; Strauss, involved with the Munich *Guntram* at the time, refused to vouchsafe a detailed programme. 'All wit spent in notes' was his explanation, and *Till Eulenspiegel* needs no further apology (though he eventually

45

provided programme notes, in a characteristically terse and witty Bavarian manner, for a 'guide' to *Till*).

It was an outstanding success: enthusiasts and suspicious adversaries alike found themselves swept along by its wonderful sense of movement, and when Debussy heard it in Paris in 1903, along with *Ein Heldenleben* and *Aus Italien*, he marvelled at Strauss's ability to organise and sustain interest in his expressive and colourful material. Hanslick would no longer be able to talk of superfluous colour, for colour had become form: *Till*'s main motifs, on horn and shrill D clarinet, exploited the potentials of their instruments in a way that rendered idea and agent inseparable, and if Strauss now dared to introduce the triple woodwind from *Guntram* in a purely orchestral work, he made sure that the newcomers had rôles to play, too. What Hanslick found to lament was that 'many charming, witty ideas spring up in the work, but not a single one that does not instantly have its neck broken by the speed with which the next one lands on its head'.

Till Eulenspiegel's 'street ditty' in a 1944 autograph copy of the score made for 'Till's 50th birthday'.

46

This, of course, was intentional sleight-of-hand: Strauss later remarked that he could rarely extend to long themes, but he knew he was a master at the endless transformation of shorter ones. There was, besides, room within the cunningly-wrought rondo form for a generous marshalling of the forces before Till's lightning-speed trial, hanging and apotheosis. The dazzling clarity of the orchestration and the humour which had been glimpsed in the *Burleske* stood revealed here in astonishing opposition to the mood of *Guntram*. There had been nothing like it in German music since Beethoven's Eighth Symphony, cited by Strauss as a model.

No sooner was *Till* rushing triumphantly from city to city across Germany, than Strauss turned almost immediately to another tone-poem which would provide the absolute contrast necessary to him. The flow of songs inspired by Pauline continued, including the famous group of Op.32 in 1896, but work on a *Singspiel* after Goethe, *Lîla*, seems to have come to a standstill around the time that Cosima began to show an interest in it. Certainly Strauss's choice of a work by Nietzsche for the subject of this next tone-poem suggests a devil-may-care attitude towards Bayreuth, worthy of Till himself.

Nietzsche, the prophet of a new aristocracy that would lead the world to new heights of progress, was now a cult figure. But Strauss's admiration for him was tainted by scepticism, and in taking the central theme of Nietzsche's *Also sprach Zarathustra* – that of man passing through various stages of religious and scientific development before emerging as the *Übermensch* (our translation lamely renders 'Superman') – he was, like Mahler and Delius shortly after him, more interested in the musical possibilities of the prose's lush imagery and sensuous appeal. Beginning work in December 1895, he selected nine chapter-headings out of Nietzsche's 80 and took them as inspiration for a free interpretation, at the same time following the earthling's struggle toward the stratosphere of *Übermensch* status.

The central musical idea, he wrote in his sketchbook, was 'the alternation between the two remotest keys': B major, and occasionally B minor, representing man, and C major representing nature. The latter gave him an opening trumpet-call of stark splendour, one of the simple *Naturthema*s using the most prominent intervals of the scale which were fast becoming his stock-in-trade, building to a climax crowned by a thundering organ chord; both keys, pitted against each other, ended the work in equally striking fashion in the unanswered question of the final bars. In between came sumptuous orchestral writing and dense counterpoint fitted to this strange subject; a passage for strings divided into sixteen parts gave hints of increasing refinement

Friedrich Nietzsche, author
of *Also sprach Zarathustra*.

towards a chamber-music style and Strauss nodded in the
direction of a 'new music' through a fugue ('Of Science and
Learning') the subject of which is made up of all twelve tones of
the chromatic scale. He was stretching harmonic and textural
tensions in a way that strikingly pre-empts Schoenberg's early
orchestral works less than a decade later. But just when it seemed
that he might be overwhelmed by the seriousness of his theme, he
deflated pretensions by marking the emergence of the *Übermensch*
with a Viennese waltz, a thing of light and joy but at the same time
delicious parody at a crucial point. Strauss conducted the
première in Frankfurt on 27 November 1896, and it was heard in
Berlin (under Nikisch, to rapturous acclaim) and Cologne within
the next few days. He wrote exuberantly to Pauline declaring it
'by far the most important of all my pieces . . . faultlessly scored'.

Although he recalled an 'unspoken but nevertheless irrevocable
separation from Wahnfried-Bayreuth' at this time, he remained
on good terms with Cosima. He was away touring his money-
spinning melodrama using Tennyson's verses, *Enoch Arden*
(op.38), a vehicle for Ernst von Possart, the Munich Intendant,

48

when his son Franz was born on 12 April 1897. Cosima sent wry congratulations on the happy event: 'Hail to the Expression family, beg not Zarathustra as teacher, offer self as governess'. Like Papa Strauss, Bülow and Ritter, she was understanding enough to realise that the young composer must make his mark as he thought best.

In the wake of his son's birth, the cheerful father sketched out new ideas in his notebook for 16 April: 'Symphonic poem *Held und Welt* (Hero and World) begins to take place; as satyr-play to accompany it – *Don Quichotte*.' The complementary relationship between what was eventually to become *Ein Heldenleben* and *Don Quixote* was always stressed by Strauss; he thought they would make an ideal concert programme together. He began work on both simultaneously, but *Don Quixote* loomed larger and pressed for immediate attention. The *donnée* this time was 'the battle of one theme against a nullity', the tone mock-heroic: 'I took variation form *ad absurdam* and showered tragicomic persiflage upon it'. The master ironist in Strauss, pulling so many different coloured strings and holding them skilfully in play, was beginning to take shape.

Wüllner was again entrusted with a Strauss première, and the first performance of *Don Quixote* took place in Cologne on 8 March 1898; Strauss conducted it in Frankfurt ten days later. Inevitably the more sensational pictorial elements (the brass-bleating sheep and Quixote's imaginary flight through the air on the wooden horse, guided by a wind machine) caused an uproar, but for all those who saw only superficial scene-painting, there were others like the French writer Romain Rolland, who heard the work in Düsseldorf the following year and found 'remarkable intelligence . . . these are really sketches . . . rather than real descriptions'. The complex design set the most detailed polyphony (justified as an expression of the protagonist's diseased mind) against sketches of glowing melody and euphony which emphasised the strain of poignant idealism and ultimate sanity. A solo cello took the rôle of Quixote, a viola that of Sancho Panza, although neither had exclusive claim on the characterisations; this was no concerto, nor even a *sinfonia concertante*, but an opera with instrumental voices, another hint at the kind of character study Strauss would soon attempt in his operas. *Don Quixote* stands among the tone-poems (as *Die Frau ohne Schatten* stands among the operas) as Strauss's most ambitious attempt to bring together and pit against each other the diverse sound-worlds with which he had so far experimented. At the same time it retains a flavour of its own as a succinct tribute to Cervantes's novel.

In addition to his Munich commitments, Strauss found time to conduct elsewhere. In addition to the Frankfurt concerts, he travelled to Vienna, Budapest, Brussels, Moscow and (in November and December of 1897) to Paris, where Pauline sang several of his songs in their orchestral versions. He also visited London, for the British première of *Tod und Verklärung* in a programme that also included Mozart's *Eine kleine Nachtmusik* and orchestral excerpts from Wagner's operas. The following April he had to refuse an invitation to give 30 operatic performances in London. He also turned down an offer of a three-year contract in Hamburg because he was promoted to chief conductor at the Munich Opera on Levi's retirement in 1896, and his salary was more substantial.

Financial considerations had to be taken into account not out of greed but because, as Pauline pointed out, if her husband wanted to devote more time to composition, he would need the money to support such work. But when a position at New York's Metropolitan Opera House was offered to him, complete with alluring wages, he turned it down in favour of a more stable situation he had been negotiating in Berlin. On 9 April 1898 he signed a ten-year contract, to begin that November, taking over most of Felix Weingartner's Berlin engagements with the exception of his Philharmonic concerts (these, too, were eventually to come under Strauss's control). So on the eve of the twentieth century, Strauss set out with his wife, son and half a 'hero' – *Ein Heldenleben* in short score, to be precise – for the centre of Prussian supremacy.

An aerial view of Berlin at the turn of the century.

50

Chapter 6

No More Heroics

Kaiser Wilhelm II

As Strauss completed the short score of *Ein Heldenleben* on 30 July 1898, he heard that another hero had withdrawn from the world. Otto von Bismarck, Chancellor of Germany until his dismissal by the wild and foolhardy Kaiser Wilhelm II in 1891, had died. After a cautious marshalling of internal forces in the wake of the victory over France in 1871, Bismarck's policies had rushed pell-mell towards expansionism in the 1880s. Germany was experiencing her greatest period of industrial and financial growth as the century drew to a close; but she was also turning her attention towards her navy and other nations, above all Britain, were becoming alarmed. Bismarck knew the dangers he had engineered when he saw the young Kaiser on the throne: in such hands these forces could go out of control. The early years of Wilhelm II's reign promised a greater liberalism, but once Bismarck had been removed, the Chancellors who followed had nothing like his power and influence, and Wilhelm's self-willed policies had no check.

Taking only a superficial look at Strauss's work at the time, it would have been easy to cast the composer in the rôle of arrogant, intoxicated spokesman of this power-hungry era. Failing to read the irony between the lines, one could draw the same conclusion today from his wry announcement to Spitzweg that, since Beethoven's *Eroica* was 'so seldom performed nowadays' he was 'composing, in order to meet a pressing need, a great tone-poem entitled *Ein Heldenleben* (true, it has no funeral march, but it *is* in E flat major and has lots of horns, which are of course well versed in heroism).' He even changed the last few bars, in December 1898, to end with a brass peroration which he described, again with tongue in cheek, to Willi Schuh in 1946 as a 'state funeral'.

This vainglorious image was, of course, very far from the truth. Romain Rolland, whose perceptive remarks on *Don Quixote* have already been touched upon in the previous chapter, was one of the few to penetrate the composer's increasingly enigmatic and seemingly indifferent façade, to discover the buffoon and master ironist that lurked beneath. Rolland's diary, changing in tone on each of his successive meetings with Strauss, suggests how long he

Strauss in 1898: the famous portrait by Fritz Erler.

The Strauss family in their Berlin apartment on the Knesebeckstrasse.

took to solve the riddle. He had first heard the composer conduct *Also sprach Zarathustra* at Lamoureux's in 1898, although it was in the militaristic environment of the 1899 Düsseldorf Music Festival that he formed an impression of Strauss as a self-willed, proud figure who was the Germans' 'poet of victory'. Yet, a year later in Paris, he had time to change his mind about Strauss. First the response is equivocal:

His conversation shows me how right I was to see in him the typical artist of the new German empire, the powerful reflection of that heroic pride, which is on the verge of becoming delirious, of that egotistical and practical idealism, which makes a cult of power and disdains weakness. In addition to this he has certain dispositions which I had not seen clearly before, and which strictly speaking belong more to the people of Munich, the south Germans: an elemental vein of the clownish humour, paradoxical and satirical, of a spoilt child, or of Till Eulenspiegel. In order not to consider some of his ideas odious, one must bear this in mind.

Strauss was in Paris to conduct several concerts, not on holiday. Yet perhaps the time he spent walking with Rolland through the boulevards and galleries of the city seems to have had an effect on him not dissimilar to the spell cast on Henry James's American 'ambassador' Lambert Strether. Strauss seems to have intrigued Rolland with a curious 'double consciousness' consisting, as James puts it of Strether, of 'detachment in his zeal and curiosity in his indifference'. Strolling through the Louvre, Rolland noticed to his surprise that Strauss seemed to despise those paintings which emphasised the tragic, the pompous or the heroic, and to show a connoisseur's taste for the 'happiness and talent for living' displayed in the works of the eighteenth century masters such as Watteau. That evening he offered Rolland a rare confidence:

. . . he says to me naïvely, nicely: 'I am not a hero, I haven't got the necessary strength; I am not cut out for battle; I prefer to withdraw, to be quiet, to have peace. I haven't enough genius. I lack the strength of health, and will-power. I don't want to overstrain myself. At the moment I need to create gentle, happy music. No more heroic things.'

Fritz Erler's portrait of the composer in 1898 shows the nervous over-excitability, which no doubt contributed towards the serious illnesses of the Weimar years, now compounded with a lassitude self-imposed, as it were, to save him unnecessary strain. For the camera he could assume any number of guises: the bourgeois, the respectable musician with the clear, candid eyes or the haunted genius. Yet the tension of opposites could not continue for ever, and although 'gentle, happy music' was not to take over for some

53

Romain Rolland

time, *Heldenleben* was in one way his farewell to the healthy exaggerations of his youth. Even there, a certain turning to advantage of the gargantuan spirit of the age (by employing forces larger than any he had used so far and applying them in many places to give massive, thick textures, which lend the work an undeniable character of its own) was offset by a characteristic humour.

Once again Strauss was anxious to suppress the 'programme' for the first performance of *Ein Heldenleben* (in Frankfurt on 3 March 1899, Strauss conducting once again), but the concert promoters requested one and Friedrich Rösch wrote an accompanying booklet to supplement the suggestive titles of the work's six sections. Inevitably the critics read it and assumed, Strauss wrote to his father, that 'the hideously-portrayed "fault-finders and adversaries" are supposed to be themselves, and the Hero me, which is only partly true'. In a lengthy and fiendishly difficult section for the principal violinist, he had certainly sketched Pauline in all her infinite variety, but, as he had told Rolland, he could never engage in battle; and there was no question of satisfied retirement. *Ein Heldenleben* was, after all, conceived as the companion-piece to *Don Quixote*, and the parody and persiflage of

Ein Heldenleben: first page of the autograph score.

those 'fantastic variations' should be allowed their appearance: German conductors and orchestras solemnise the benevolent energy of the striding opening and the return from battle at their peril. The wit is cruder and starker than in *Till* or *Zarathustra*, extending even to the battle (when did a real warmonger swing into action in anything other than march time?), but Strauss never wanted to tread again over old territory. Serene idylls appear not only when we expect them, but also in that apparently impossible task of self-quotation in the Works of Peace section: no less than 31 examples of Strauss's best inventions so far woven convincingly into a rich tapestry. These were the elements which combined to enthrall Debussy and left him marvelling at the way in which one's interest was held, through so many disparate images, from first to last. *Ein Heldenleben* was decidedly the work of the unpredictable figure whom Rolland saw, to his surprise, bulkily execute an *entrechat* across a Parisian salon.

The only politics which concerned Strauss at this time were those of the Berlin Court Opera where he was conductor-in-chief. For him the contrast was less the one between Bavarian *Gemütlichkeit* and Prussian inflexibility so often stressed by historians, than between the frustrations of the Munich mire and the freedom of musical Berlin. He was prepared to endure for Berlin's sake the philistinism of the operatic audiences, the conservative Kaiser with his distaste for everything modern and – for the time being – the increasingly restrictive censorship laws. His reputation shielded him from the problems experienced by conductors in less exalted positions, such as Bruno Walter (who was to remember how he had groaned under the painful yoke of the Opera's bureaucracy). Strauss and Pauline seldom socialised and his response to the Kaiser was one of carefully veiled disapproval, with some lip-service later in the form of military marches. Commitments to a wide operatic repertory kept him fully occupied: Wagner still occupied a prominent place, with *Tristan* to celebrate his inauguration in Berlin and a Wagner Festival soon afterwards, and he made sure that Charpentier's *Louise* and Bizet's *Carmen* became established favourites. He continued to travel, and before taking up his post he conducted the Amsterdam Concertgebouw Orchestra in *Also sprach Zarathustra*, which he described in his diary as 'best performance the work has yet had, greatest triumph'. As a thanksgiving tribute, he dedicated *Ein Heldenleben* to the Amsterdam players.

Between *Ein Heldenleben* and the next major work came no less than 33 songs and various pieces for male voice choir. The present situation called for no comment. Another burden from the past, however, had still to be exorcised. Neither *Till Eulenspiegel* nor *Don Quixote* had shocked the mutton-headed Munich burghers as

Strauss at the time of taking up the Berlin residency.

56

Strauss had hoped. What better revenge could there be for their cruel 'slaughter' of young *Guntram* than a second opera in a vein quite different from the first, with a sting in the tail for the *Müncheners*?

That something lighter would follow the Wagnerian *Guntram* had not been in doubt. Both the *Lîla* project and a ballet with a scenario based on Watteau's *L'Embarquement pour Cythère* were to contain 'old-fashioned, modish rococo elements . . . the aura of moonshine', as he had written to Cosima in 1895. When Strauss later exploited this style in *Ariadne auf Naxos* and the incidental music to Hofmannsthal's adaptation of *Le Bourgeois Gentilhomme*, he did not forget the sketches for *Cythère*. But it was the satirist and founder of the *Überbrettl* cabaret movement, Ernst von Wolzogen, who in 1899 rekindled Strauss's enthusiasm in this direction by tempting him with a humorous sally against the citizens of Munich. He would be delighted to oblige with a libretto, since he too had suffered disappointment and rejection with his experimental cabaret in Munich (and he too had had better luck in the more receptive artistic climate of Berlin). The source he proposed was the Flemish legend *The Extinguished Fires of Oudenarde*. In it, a magician helps a young lover take revenge on a maiden who has made him the laughing-stock of the town when she promised to haul him up to her bedroom in a basket and left him hanging there midway. The nature of the revenge, whereby the magician extinguishes the fires of the town and announces that they can only be rekindled by a flame from the girl's backside as she stands naked in the market-place, had to be altered in the libretto, but the substitute ending suited Strauss well: the girl would yield up her virginity and the lights of love and inspiration would be restored.

Wolzogen eagerly sketched the libretto during a few blissful summer days in 1900. The emphasis, Strauss insisted, should be on 'the brazen, burlesque element', and the centrepiece was to be the hero's monologue on light and love. Despite the complications of covert references to Wagner (the absent master-magician – also 'driven out' from Munich, where the action was now set – just as Strauss could be seen as the apprentice), the score of *Feuersnot* (Fire-famine) could be simple and melodic enough to delight his father with its folksong kinship to *Till Eulenspiegel*. Strauss completed the full score, aptly enough, on Wagner's birthday in 1901.

After the meandering construction of *Guntram*, *Feuersnot* was cast in a one-act form, the first of Strauss's operas to apply the lessons of symphonic form (and, as in *Till*, the woodwind have most of the best lines, though the rôles of Kunrad and Diemut are fine challenges for a high baritone and soprano who can act

Ernst von Schuch, conductor of the first performances of *Feuersnot, Salome, Elektra* and *Der Rosenkavalier*.

convincingly). *Feuersnot* is never dull; despite its topicality, with an abundance of untranslatable puns in Munich dialect, its good humour transcends the location and it moves with tremendous spirit towards its resolution in Kunrad's and Diemut's love-scene, a satisfying musical and dramatic synthesis of the opera's major themes in which the voices play only a small part. 'That a love scene?' wrote Colette when she heard it performed as a concert extract in Paris. 'My God, if I went into such tumultuous ecstasies I'd be afraid of what my neighbours downstairs might say! The programme was right: a "scene" it was, not a duet. One would have thought there were fifteen of them, not just two.' Her friend Debussy cautioned that without knowing the context it was fair to conjecture whether such 'orchestral torrents' were not after all justified by the text. As the crowning glory of the work, they undoubtedly were. In *Der Rosenkavalier* there would be another love-scene, briefer and still more graphic; and the waltzes which populate *Feuersnot* so beguilingly would proliferate in Strauss's second comedy.

59

Ernst von Schuch, who had impressed Strauss with a performance of *Till Eulenspiegel* in December 1895, conducted the première of *Feuersnot* on 21 November 1901 at the Dresden Court Opera, where he had been general musical director since 1882. In gratitude for Schuch's success, Strauss was to ensure that Dresden had the pick of future operatic first performances. Elsewhere, *Feuersnot* soon ran into censorship difficulties: the offstage consummation and a handful of ribald verses on its likelihood had offended official sensibilities. In Berlin it received only a handful of performances before the Kaiserin objected and the run was discontinued. As director of the Vienna Court Opera, Mahler campaigned vigorously for Viennese acceptance and conducted the opera several times to great acclaim, although Alma Mahler claimed incorrectly in her memoirs that Mahler shunned *Feuersnot* because he had an 'absolute horror' of the piece. Indeed, much in her account of the Strausses' behaviour at the Vienna

Gustav Mahler

première on 29 January 1902 is to be treated with caution. Pauline, she asserted, ranted to her about the mediocrity of her husband's opera (though in a later chapter of her memoirs, Alma says that she only ever met 'the de Ahna woman' once, and not on this occasion); and Strauss spent the whole time calculating his profits.

To what extent, in fact, Strauss became obsessed by moneymaking is hard to tell. Alma was not the only observer to criticise his love of gain. There can be no doubt that he showed a more than average concern for collecting his fees and royalties, but he also held a realistic appraisal of a composer's precarious existence, and he took steps to improve conditions for others. Composers had long suffered the tyranny of the publisher and the knowledge that their personal rights over their work expired shortly after they did: were they not, then, entitled to the privileges which poets and novelists already held? In 1898 Strauss instigated a campaign in which 160 composers were asked for their views on the subject, and at a conference that September he set out his views on the protection of performing rights. A resolution was passed in favour of a new composers' guild, the *Genossenschaft Deutscher Tonsetzer*, though it was not until 1903 in Berlin that the association was able to put any of its plans into action. Mahler, being freed from the restraint of a Viennese organisation, was one of the first to benefit.

However indifferent generally to the outside world, Strauss could not do enough in the service of music. In 1901 he became President of the *Allgemeine Deutscher Musikverein* and his work there in establishing new works, regardless of their composers' countries of origin, showed a breadth of appreciation which more than atoned for his fervent denunciations on non-Germans when he had been under the Wagnerian spell. Now it was different: Chabrier, D'Indy and Magnard fared well under Strauss's encouragement at the ADM Festivals, along with the Third and Fourth Symphonies of Mahler. At the 1902 Festival in Düsseldorf Strauss praised Elgar for his *Dream of Gerontius* and in his speech on the day after the second performance, described Elgar as being among the vanguard of British composers, establishing Elgar's reputation in Germany. Bruno Walter, who had also had several works accepted by the ADM, wrote in his autobiography that 'the selection of contemporary works of the most divergent tendencies and styles gave a thoroughly favourable impression of the committee's open-mindedness'. For Strauss, whose only demand was that composers should be 'true and genuine children of your own times', the teeming forms of musical life around the turn of the century all had some validity. He put his eclectic judgement to good use when it came to helping others.

Chapter 7

Riding the Storm

In 1902 Strauss returned to Britain, giving concerts in London, Birmingham, Glasgow and Edinburgh, and the following year he shared conducting honours with Willem Mengelberg (joint dedicatee with his Amsterdam players of *Ein Heldenleben*) in a Strauss Festival at London's St James's Hall. After these concerts with the Concertgebouw Orchestra, he took a holiday on the Isle of Wight with Pauline and their son Franz, and there he completed the sketch of his next tone-poem, the *Symphonia Domestica*, under circumstances congenial to this half-idyllic, half-comic representation of his family life. The sun shone every day, and the 6-year-old 'Bubi', a merry child and already making progress in piano lessons with the proud father, played delightedly on the beaches at Sandown. This was not an image that found its way into the work (the 'child at play' scherzo had already been completed), though it raises uncomfortable parallels with Mahler's near-contemporary nightmare of fate dogging the

Two images of Strauss in 1902: a photograph of the composer at home and a lithograph from the *Berliner Musik- und Theaterzeitung* referring to the famous portrayal of the critics in *Ein Heldenleben*: 'The hero's enemies'.

New York, Fifth Avenue, circa 1900.

children who zig-zag through the sand in the trio of his Sixth Symphony's second movement. The outcome and the frame of reference could not be further removed from Mahler's chilling prophecy of his daughter's untimely death. For Strauss, the *Symphonia Domestica* was an exuberant, mock-epic celebration of his happy household, and some saw an alarming opportunism in his offering the first performance to the Americans, ready for his first visit to the USA at the beginning of 1904.

Completion of a ballad on the Battle of Hastings for choir and a huge orchestra of 145 players, *Taillefer*, intervened (it was ready for the centenary of Heidelberg University in October 1903), but the orchestration of the 'symphony' was ready just before Strauss and his wife left Berlin for the States. The first performance took place in Carnegie Hall on 21 March 1904 with Strauss conducting players gathered together as a new orchestra by the man who was funding his appearances at great expense, Hermann Hans Wetzler. 'After a great deal of annoyance by that band of anarchists, the New York musicians, I obtained a brilliant

63

Formal domesticity: Strauss, Franz and Pauline.

performance following 15 rehearsals' he wrote to his father, passing over the problems the occasion caused. For if the affluent New Yorkers had paid a great deal for a Strauss première, the work's reception cost the composer still dearer: much as he tried to keep the programme secret, news of the details leaked out and the press mercilessly seized on superficial guidelines instead of listening to the music ('Papa and Momma and Baby Celebrated in Huge Conglomeration of Orchestral Music' read part of one typically verbose headline). He had undoubtedly made a bad choice if he hoped for a sympathetic reception of this unusual work with its fair share of irony and flippancy. Infuriated by the hounding of the press, Strauss mocked one very persistent lady by stating that a particular moment in *Domestica* portrayed him standing on the balcony in shirt-sleeves!

Autobiography, Strauss insisted, was second nature to every artist. 'Chevalley advises me against always composing myself' he wrote to Bernhard Schuster in 1905. 'Do you know a composer who has ever composed anything but himself? Funny people, these aestheticians!' Rolland, judicious as always, warned Strauss not to print the 'programme' of the work for its performance in Paris (inadvertently, and adversely for the work's fate in the States,

64

Strauss had left in telling details in the score, such as the cries of the aunts and uncles – 'ganz die Mama' and 'ganz der Papa' – above the orchestral parts). The Frenchman admitted afterwards that he had been shocked by the outline of this 24-hour household survey, but when he heard the performance he thought it 'perfect and unified'. He was only echoing Strauss's own words when he said that it was not the facts but the 'powerful internal forces' setting them in motion which mattered; what, Strauss asked, could be more serious than married life?

Of all the tone poems, *Symphonia Domestica* remains the most ridiculed and neglected: as Michael Kennedy rightly points out, it is absurd that the portrait of a writer's or an artist's life should be accepted in their work and ridiculed in the case of a composer. Perhaps the only commonplaces of the work are the opening themes of father, mother and child, but they lend themselves ideally to every manner of dazzling transformation and variation. The seemingly spontaneous, lucidly scored blend of lyricism and humour (Strauss's avowed intention here) is immediately struck in the child's scherzo; time and again the orchestral force of 110 is slimmed down to produce the most transparent effects. Even the climaxes, deliberately overtaxed in a nervously wrought family quarrel (double fugue) and prolonged glorification of the child to conclude, keep a massive benevolence which cannot fail to thrill in the concert hall. Rolland, who always admired the finale but at first found the polyphony overwrought, came to hold *Domestica* in esteem above all Strauss's other works. In 1926 he still found what he had called a 'joy and breadth such as you have rarely attained, and which I can find nowhere else in contemporary music'. It was, he said, the true heir of Beethoven and of Wagner's *Die Meistersinger*.

Yet joyful expressions of personal happiness were quite against the spirit of an age neurotically spoiling for conflict, and it probably suited Strauss's love of change quite well for him to turn to the unhappiest of families for his next subject. On the recommendation of the poet Anton Lindner he had seen Max Reinhardt's 1902 Berlin production of Oscar Wilde's *Salomé*, with the sensational actress Gertrud Eysoldt in the title role. The spectacle of a lascivious stepfather, a jealous harridan of a mother and an adolescent daughter brought up in an atmosphere of stifling decadence must have struck an extreme contrast to the topic of his concurrent tone-poem. Another powerful prompting was his desire to conjure the magic of the east in 'shot-silk cadences' and to dispense with the pseudo-orientalisms which he had found so inadequate in music after his return from Egypt (a good example of these can be found in Florent Schmitt's ballet *La Tragédie de Salomé*, composed after Strauss's handling of the tale).

Oscar Wilde

65

An illustration by Aubrey
Beardsley to Wilde's *Salomé*.

Wilde's prose, with its recurring phrases ideal for operatic
treatment, almost set itself to music, so Lindner's offer of a
libretto proved unnecessary. However stilted a poet Strauss may
have been in *Guntram*, he knew unerringly here which portions of
the play to use, where music should serve for text, and where
Wilde's lengthy expositions and distinctly elaborate syntax could
be shorn.

The score took Strauss a mere two years to complete, and in
spite of his foreign tours and the heavy schedule in Berlin,
rehearsals began in Dresden in the autumn of 1905. Immediately
there was trouble, though he must have expected it and even
seems rather to have enjoyed an uproar reminiscent of the

response to his first symphonic poems. Salome, he said, should be a 16-year-old princess with all the chastity he had noted in oriental women; so she should be slim and agile, but she should also have the voice of an Isolde. For the première, he had to settle for the voice alone: Marie Wittich – otherwise 'Auntie' in Strauss's cruel asides – was formidable both in figure and in manner. Realising that the opera was at least twice as difficult as *Feuersnot*, Strauss insisted that she needed three months to learn the part, but Ernst von Schuch, the conductor, mitigated this necessity. When, with one month left before the first performance, Wittich saw for the first time at an initial rehearsal the enormity of her task, she encouraged a deputation from the other members of the cast to hand back their parts ('I won't do it, I'm a decent woman', she fulminated). They were shamed by Carl Burrian, the Herod, who declared that he knew the rôle already. Even so, the first performance had to be moved back from November to December.

Strauss had some inkling of the sensation his opera would provoke. He had been reluctant to play it through to a horrified Cosima, and his father gave characteristic comment: 'Oh God, what nervous music. It is exactly as if one had one's trousers full of maybugs.' Franz, however, died on 31 May 1905, aged 85, and was spared the occasion of the *Salome* première on 9 December,

One of the last photographs of Strauss together with his father.

when this most progressive of his son's works so far was greeted by 38 curtain calls – and the denunciation of the conservative press. Franz had witnessed each of Richard's works with increasing disapproval, but he had never once prevented him from finding his own voice. Perhaps he thought that the persistent advice of his letters would somehow take effect; had he lived even longer, he might have seen that his influence reached farther than he believed.

Salome's reputation spread immediately; as Sir Thomas Beecham pointed out in *A Mingled Chime*, 'whenever there is the slightest hint of naughtiness in a piece, the whole town yearns to see it.' Dresden, where *Feuersnot* had first been performed, was a wise choice for the première, since censorship difficulties fell elsewhere. Even so Strauss had justifiably, if mistakenly, surmised that if Wilde could slip through the bureaucrats' net, so too could Wilde set to music. He was wrong. For the London performance, conducted by Sir Thomas Beecham during his second Covent Garden season in 1910 (after the successes of *Elektra* and *Feuersnot*), the Lord Chancellor had demanded certain 'modifications' in the text to suit New Testament decorum: Salome's desire for Jokanaan, for example, was to be expressed nonsensically as religious fervour. Elgar in America was asked to lead meetings to pray for the failure of this sacrilegious opera. In Berlin, the Kaiser allowed *Salome* to appear on condition that the star of Bethlehem should be seen twinkling optimistically at the end. He had been trapped into accepting the cacophony of his 'bosom-viper' because he had himself suggested to Strauss that he write an opera on Herod. The depravity of *Salome*, in fact, unwittingly paralleled the cabinet scandals of the next few years, culminating in the Hülsen-Haeseler affair, when the Count of that name, chief of the military ministry, danced in a pink ballet-skirt at the home of Prince Fürstenberg before dropping down dead. Such tokens of a Germany hurtling towards catastrophe satisfied the public appetite with astonishing regularity.

Mahler, who had given the first Viennese performance of *Symphonia Domestica*, battled in vain against civic narrow-mindedness to gain *Salome* a place at the State Opera; his failure and his anger contributed to his resignation from the Directorship in 1907. Admiration for the opera led him only to increased perplexity at the enigma of Strauss's character. The two men were growing further apart in their attitudes; for Mahler, Strauss's equivocal nature and his streak of opportunism were incompatible with his genius as a composer. Perhaps their mutual incomprehension is best expressed in Strauss's response to a comment of Mahler's, written in the margin of Mahler's (published)

The Scottish soprano, Mary Garden, as Salome in 1912.

diary. Bewildered, he queried: 'Are people made of different stuff than I?' To which Strauss pencilled in an emphatic 'Yes!!!' Mahler's music was intensely autobiographical; so too was Strauss's, but in a different way. His ironic distancing over the years enabled him to enter other worlds and inject them with something of his own, or to infuse his self-portraits with a little parody and self-mockery. What seemed like cold calculation to Mahler was self-preservation to Strauss (in 1906, Alma records that Strauss told Mahler to 'look after himself better. No-one would give him anything for wearing himself out. A pig sty that wouldn't even put on *Salome* – no, it wasn't worth it!'). It must

Two caricatures of Strauss
and *Salome*: silhouette by
Bithorn and Garvens'
'Offering to the critics'.

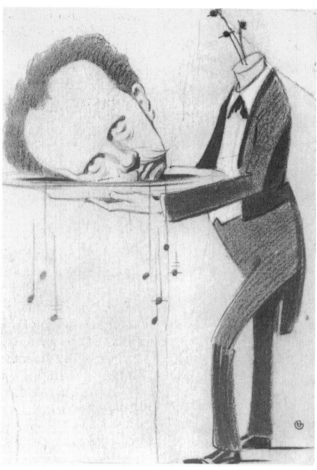

however, also be remembered that what seemed like unbridled egotism and squandering of energy to Strauss produced some of the most intense autobiography in symphonic form. Musically, neither view is exclusive to the other, but nor could the creators continue to meet on a comfortable middle ground.

In a letter to Alma in 1907, Mahler recorded his high esteem of *Salome*:

Deeply at work in it, under a mass of rubble, is a live volcano, a subterranean fire – not a mere firework! It is probably the same with Strauss's whole personality. That is what makes it so hard to separate the wheat from the chaff in him. But I have enormous respect for the phenomenon as a whole, and have now reaffirmed it. I am immensely glad.

There were many who thought that Strauss had abandoned the path of sanity for unbridled modernism altogether. Yet there is little in *Salome* which suggests effect for effect's sake; simply a perfect matching of colour and theme to characterisation. The glittering grace of Salome's music before her desire turns, thwarted, to perversity, is not so far from the harp-spangled dreams of the sleeping family in *Symphonia Domestica*. Against it Jokanaan warns and prophesies in a more simply diatonic style, richly and more heavily orchestrated – though there is a suggestion that his visions of doom do as much harm to the impressionable princess as anything, or anyone, in Herod's court (Strauss was out of sympathy with this man of God and confessed that he ended up by thoroughly disliking him). Salome's increasing obsession, verging on madness, had its precedent in Don Quixote's delirium, and the depths to which her perverted passions sink are represented, with a literal but masterly stroke, by the contrabassoon taking over her luminous clarinet theme of the opera's opening bars, as she leans over the cistern. The squabbling of the religious factions and Herod's final desperation are the few instances where harmonic tension is stretched to the brink of atonality, but the final goal, essentially a rich scena for the soprano, brings a classical resolution and with it a terrible longing for what might have been. One effect – the double basses' persistent jabs in the near-silence of Salome's wait for the severed head – had to be softened by a sustained cor anglais note at Dresden, since it was considered offensive. Generally, Strauss avoided the purely graphic and his avowed intent of evoking the atmosphere of the east without crude exoticisms was carefully observed – except, perhaps, in the *Dance of the Seven Veils* which he had left until the rest had been completed.

Rolland, who played a large part in preparing this latest Strauss work for Parisian audiences by assisting with the nuances of a

French translation, held significant reservations. His analogy for *Salome* was a river of flowing lava sweeping the listener along irresistibly, but he felt that Strauss's absorption in decadent literature was unwholesome. His reasons are crucial in the light of the composer's subsequent development:

The impression I have of you (I am perhaps mistaken) is that you are essentially lyrical. The only thing you *feel* with genius is your own personality (and everything that resembles it, either closely or remotely). As you have, besides your genius, great intelligence and will-power, you are always capable of *understanding* other passions or other characters, but from the outside, without feeling them really deeply, on your own account.

And he concludes:

You have triumphed over the Europe of our times. Now you must leave our Europe, raise yourself above it. There is, in the European world today, an unbridled force of decadence, of suicide – (in various forms, in Germany, in France) – beware of joining forces with it. Let that which must die, die, – and live yourself.

In his way of life, Strauss now took one significant step away from contemporary Europe. With the royalties from *Salome*, he fashioned for his family a mountain retreat: the villa at Garmisch-Partenkirchen, in the valley of the River Loisach south of Munich. His youthful Alpine expeditions had given him a profound feeling for the beauties of nature, and the holidays in Italy, Greece and Egypt made him long for the warmth of the sun. The Garmisch villa offered ample scope for both, and his working pattern came increasingly to depend on the spring and early summer months, when he could choose to be free from conducting engagements. He explained in his old age:

Cherry trees do not blossom in the winter, and no more are musical ideas born when nature is bleak and cold. I am a great nature lover. Therefore it is to be expected that I should do my best creative work amid the Bavarian mountains in the spring.

Earlier, in response to a questionnaire on artistic creativity, he had stressed the need for isolation and replied that good ideas often occurred to him on afternoon walks; the rest took place in the meticulously ordered atmosphere of the Garmisch study. His working methods were highly methodical, and his pencil sketches, piano scores and full scores contained very few crossings-out. He began the full score at the top and worked downwards (with many composers the opposite was the case, for reasons of accurate orchestration and harmony); this way, he said, he ran less risk of smudging the ink. 'I am never feverishly excited', he wrote about scoring. 'One must be master of oneself in order to keep that ever-changing, ever-moving chessboard called the orchestra under control. The mind that composed *Tristan* must have been as cold as marble.' There is no better answer to those detractors of Strauss who claim that such detachment was inhuman. Yet Strauss felt, too, that industry alone was not sufficient for creativity, and only on rare occasions of compulsion in later years would he manufacture music if the inspiration was lacking.

No doubt Strauss now wanted to turn back to the happier *Feuersnot/Domestica* mood most suited to his serene surroundings. What channelled his energies back to the spirit of the age was an arresting offer from a playwright whom, he intuitively surmised, would be the lifelong operatic collaborator he was seeking. Quelling reservations, he took the most important step of all for his future as an opera composer.

The villa at Garmisch.

Chapter 8

Tragical . . . Comical

During those same few days in Paris when Rolland was amiably fathoming the riddle of Strauss's character, the Viennese poet and playwright Hugo von Hofmannsthal approached the composer with the proposal for a ballet scenario. It was an abortive move; when he followed up the suggestion with a written draft of the scenario, he received a genial refusal. With typical clear-sightedness Strauss explained that much as he admired the poetical content of what he had perused, he had his own ballet project (*Cythère*) to deal with for the moment, and that after his next opera (*Feuersnot*) it would be time to turn back to symphonic form. Yet careful planning eventually yielded to inspirational impulse after Strauss saw Hofmannsthal's 'new version' of Sophocles' *Electra* in Berlin in November 1903 – again produced by Max Reinhardt in Berlin and again with Gertrud Eysoldt as the vengeful princess.

In a sense *Elektra* was as extreme an example of Hofmannsthal's poetic thinking as *Salome* had been of the nervous strain in Strauss's fundamentally congenial, robust nature. Both the play and the opera posited a disintegration of the values their creators cherished. Hofmannsthal, born in 1874 into a Viennese aristocracy that celebrated aestheticism in art that was ornate and sensuous, later pointed out that he was nourished on a heritage that had much in common with the composer's Bavarian 'Rococo'. At the same time, dark forces which had hardly touched Munich were already manifest in *fin-de-siècle* Vienna, and they begged a deeper response. With the coming to power of the Christian Socialists, led by the virulently anti-Semitic Karl Lüger, in 1895, liberalism was threatened and its artistic representatives mostly took the same course: they retreated, like many of the Pre-Raphaelites in Victorian England, into a fantasy world. Hofmannsthal rejected this enchanted garden and dedicated himself to the problem of synthesis – of grasping the complexity of the contemporary world and infusing it with one's own artistic vision. In *Der Tor und der Tod* (1893) and *Der Tod des Tizians* (1894) he used allegory to express the dilemma. It was only in later years that he felt confident enough to establish a wider symbolic framework in which any kind of optimistic resolution

Hugo von Hofmannsthal

was possible (then the dissatisfied wife of a Greek blacksmith in one of the early poems, speared by her unimaginative husband as she tries to flee into a centaur's promised world of unbridled impulse, became Barak's wife in *Die Frau ohne Schatten*, saved from a similar fate by superhuman intervention). For the moment, the writer was caught between the dangerous extremes of brute instinct and stultifying subordination to a political creed. Like his compatriot, Robert Musil, the Austrian author of the three-volume novel *Der Mann ohne Eigenschaften* (The Man Without Qualities), Hofmannsthal saw man as living in an age of endless choices, endless uncertainty – a society dwelling on a shifting glacier. This sense of instability he called *das Gleiternde*.

Hoffmannsthal's reinterpretation of the Electra myth took the situation down into an abyss: human ideals had been demolished to such an extent that the only surgery possible was the knife. Freud, whose early case-histories in collaboration with Josef Breuer and analysis of dreams, *Die Traumdeutung* (The Interpretation of Dreams), had already appeared, contributed much to the new image of Elektra as an hysteric traumatised by the loss of her father and consumed with hatred for her murderess-mother; her libido had been entirely channelled into a desire for revenge. Without the necessary resolution of childhood sexuality, instinct ran amok; but on another level the ritual killing of Clytemnestra and Aegisthus – the womanish lover who had helped her kill her husband – remained a justifiable and even a triumphant solution. When Strauss, inevitably attracted to this Nietzschean brand of demonic Hellenism, tried to resist a subject so close to the mood of *Salome*, Hofmannsthal countered with the observation that whereas the colours of the eastern opera had been 'purple and violet', the victory of Electra and Orestes would be light after dark, bright after black. His attitude to the matricide was as ambivalent as that of Sophocles or Euripides – or for that matter, as the questions raised by Shakespeare's contribution to the genre of the revenge-tragedy, *Hamlet*.

Attracted to Hofmannsthal as a librettist but still unsure of his *Elektra*, Strauss toyed throughout 1906 with alternative subjects for the new writer: a version of the Semiramis tale, with plenty of opportunity for ballet and spectacle; *Saul and David* after Rückert; 'an entertaining Renaissance subject' such as Savonarola or Cesare Borgia; or even something about the French Revolution. None of these bloody thoughts, in fact, seem to indicate that his mind was running along lines so different from *Elektra*; nor did any, save *Semiramis*, remotely interest Hofmannsthal. Finally Strauss capitulated to the original plan. Hofmannsthal set about adapting his play and though he made no efforts to subordinate it to an imagined musical framework, it struck Strauss as the ideal text to compose. 'You are a born librettist', he wrote, nearing the completion of the opera in July 1908, 'the greatest compliment in my opinion since I consider it much more difficult to write a good operatic text than a fine play.' Increasing commitments both in Berlin, where Weingartner finally relinquished his hold on the Berlin Philharmonic Orchestra to Strauss in April 1908, and elsewhere in Europe (in 1907 Strauss gave 31 concerts in the same number of days), prevented a swift conception of the opera. For the 1908-9 season, however, Strauss took a year's sabbatical leave from his duties, and completed *Elektra* in Garmisch on 22 September 1908.

Schuch, who had conducted *Salome*, was also to conduct the new work and was kept informed of progress. Soon rehearsals

Set design by Alfred Roller for the first production of *Elektra*, 1909.

began in Dresden. This time he came in for much more criticism from the composer. In his reminiscences Strauss recorded that Schuch's conducting lacked incisiveness. He also remarked that the orchestra was too discreet, by which he must have meant that their discretion was of the pallid variety; for there are many witnesses, among them Otto Klemperer, to claim that Strauss himself conducted the score as if it were fairy music by Mendelssohn or an operetta by Lortzing. That, at any rate, gives a rather different picture from the one often reported of the agitated composer during rehearsals bellowing from the stalls to the orchestra, 'Louder! Louder! I can still hear the singers!' Strauss's attitude was to change dramatically to one of scrupulous concern for the balance between voices and orchestra in the years to come. He was, however, satisfied with the balances and orchestral detail when the first night arrived on 25 January 1909, with Annie Krull as the eponymous heroine cavorting to more convincing dramatic effect than Marie Wittich had as Salome.

Audience reaction at Dresden was surprisingly muted, though there were enough listeners to find the 'cacophony' unworthy of comment. As the opera reached Vienna and Milan within the next few months, controversy raged over the violence and dissonance in *Elektra*. Hermann Bahr, the Viennese playwright who was to play a crucial role in Strauss's 'domestic opera' *Intermezzo*, had left the première disturbed but exhilarated. He sensed the pull towards some kind of diatonic order in spite of all the harmonic

77

'"Electrocution" by the musical headsman': woodcut caricature from the *Lustige Blätter*.

volatility which had taken the vocabulary of *Salome* one stage further. Once again Strauss had used his interplay of styles to set a core of poignant nostalgia for a happier past against the nervous instability of the divided family; he unleashed it in full force at exactly the point, some three-quarters of the way through the opera, where the psychological screw had been twisted to breaking point. The recognition of the long-absent Orestes by his sister Elektra was a crucial moment in all the Greek versions of the myth, and for Strauss it carried vital structural significance in a form as neatly symmetrical as Sophocles' own. 'I need a great moment of repose after Elektra's first shout: "Orest!"', he had told Hofmannsthal in June 1908. 'Your first consignment of lines received with thanks, but rather few. I must have material here to work at will towards a climax.'

He soon received the extra lines he wanted, and the result was Elektra's great E flat major aria, tender and heartbreaking, the briefest ray of sunshine in the storm. Strauss used the wide-

78

ranging intervals of the vocal line and strings uniquely divided, as throughout the opera, to create an impression which none of the pounding rhythms or lurid and occasionally contrived key changes, which swept the opera towards Elektra's final death-dance of victory, could quite efface. All the same the orchestral means to establish the suffocating atmosphere in Mycenae were larger even than those of *Salome*, and included among the 108 players weird and baleful contributions from a heckelphone (bass oboe – which he had introduced in *Salome*), two basset horns and a panoply of bass-heavy brass instruments: an intensification of the sombre tones of *Tod und Verklärung* and *Macbeth* used to underline the monumental starkness and shock of Greek drama. It was a world away from the sensual Palestinian night of its predecessor. Sensational graphic effects, such as the scurrying of cellos, basses and contrabassoon as Elektra digs for the buried axe or the shrilly insidious woodwind following the footsteps of the Queen's confidante and train-bearer, fitted seamlessly into an unerringly paced symphonic movement and alongside the distinctly profound terror of moments such as Klytämnestra's dream – a pasty monster oozing from the depths of the orchestra.

A restless Europe reeling and pitching towards war found that the opera sated its appetite for novelty. Sir Thomas Beecham wrote in his autobiography that the London of 1910 'was in just the right mood for a new musical sensation; it expected and got it'. Beecham became a firm ally of Strauss's when the composer came over to conduct two performances of *Elektra* on 12 and 15 March of that year. Half way through the first rehearsal Strauss stopped, finding he had nothing more to add to Beecham's already meticulous drilling of the Covent Garden orchestra. His economical gestures, memorably described by the critic of the *Daily Mail* as akin to those of 'a mathematician writing a formula on an imaginary blackboard, neatly and with supreme knowledge', were in marked contrast to the flamboyant style Rolland had noticed still very much in evidence four years earlier. The public were wildly enthusiastic about the performance, though Anglo-Saxon outrage prevailed in the musical establishment. One well-known composer, Beecham recalled, blustered that he was '"going home at once to play the chord of C major twenty times over in order to satisfy myself that it still exists."' 'The curious thing about this little piece of criticism,' Beecham added drily 'is that *Elektra* actually finishes with the chord in question, thundered out several times in repetition on the full orchestra.' Ernest Newman's smug and unspecific tirades in *The Nation* provoked an acid letter from George Bernard Shaw, who had not seen the opera but who took the opportunity to lambast the critic's arrogance as 'idiotic' because 'he unhesi-

Strauss the conductor: caricature by Bithorn.

tatingly places the judgment of the writer above that of one whom he admits to be a greater authority than himself'. When Shaw did witness *Elektra* he denounced Newman still more fervently (provoking him, incidentally, to a more detailed and balanced response), and wrote that the work represented a victorious stand against cancerous evil:

. . . the power with which it is done is not the power of the evil itself; but of the passion that detests and must and can finally destroy that evil – [that] is what makes the work great, and makes us rejoice in its horror.

Der Neurosenkavalier.

A suggestion of Strauss as neurasthenic in a topical cartoon of 1911.

For some, it was not Elektra's ambivalent victory but Klytämnestra's nightmare that became the path to follow, a state pushed to its horrifying extreme by Schoenberg in his psychodrama *Erwartung*, written the year after *Elektra*. Schoenberg was to acknowledge Strauss's crucial influence in what he called 'the emancipation of the dissonance', but he was wounded by the older composer's attitude to his own dismembering of tonal harmony. Largely untouched by the personal crises and traumas which shaped Schoenberg's musical thought and pushed it away from the late romantic style of the tone-poem *Pelléas und Mélisande* and parts of *Gurrelieder*, Strauss saw no criterion for 'progress' save the dictates of one's conscience. 'Modern?' he once exclaimed, 'what does modern mean? Give the word a different significance, have ideas like Beethoven's, write contrapuntally like Bach, orchestrate like Mozart and be true and genuine children of your own times, then you will be modern.' Now, at a turning point in musical history, he felt that he had exerted his will power to the limit in the struggle to understand the neurasthenic temperament; it was time to indulge his own lyric talent more extensively.

Strauss followed Rolland's advice to leave behind a dying Europe and searched around for a comedy even before Elektra had danced her last. Hofmannsthal's suggestion of a Casanova farce, *Cristinas Heimreise*, seemed just the opportunity to indulge his love of Mozart with the spur of a Figaro-like plot. Hofmannsthal, however, allowed the play to go beyond operatic proportions and broke his word of honour by putting it on the stage before a note could be composed. Strauss took this in good part, knowing that from Hofmannsthal alone would come the text he had been waiting for. Prior to the *Elektra* première they had established guidelines for an older form of opera with 'numbers' and *parlando* (quasi-conversational) passages corresponding to Mozart's *secco* recitative, and the writer racked his brains for a worthy subject.

The subject finally came to Hofmannsthal in February 1909, whilst he was staying with his friend Count Harry Kessler in

Weimar. Poet and polymath between them uncovered the bare bones of a plot, described in a letter to Strauss on 11 February as containing:

burlesque situations and characters, with lively action, pellucid almost like a pantomime . . . It contains two big parts, one for baritone and another for a graceful girl dressed up as a man, *à la* Farrar or Mary Garden. Period: the old Vienna under the Empress Maria Theresa.

Though this revised setting would indulge his own penchant for reconstructing the historical detail of his native city in the eighteenth century, the characters came from three French sources. Molière's protagonist in *Monsieur Pourceaugnac* became the baritone (subsequently bass) rôle, comic country-cousin Ochs, while the fussing father Geronte in the same writer's *Les Fourberies de Scapin* became the *nouveau-riche* Faninal; and Louvret de Couvray's *Les Amours du Chevalier de Faublas* provided most of the plot and the more well-bred characters – Octavian (the breeches part), the young, innocent Sophie and a Marquise, translated to Vienna as the Marschallin (intended at this stage as a minor figure). The rest was plucked from among the wealth of detail in Hogarth's engravings, from a Viennese

Plate Four of Hogarth's *Marriage à la mode*, source of inspiration for the *levée* scene in Act One of *Der Rosenkavalier*.

81

pantomime (for the intrigue at the inn), and from the cauldron of three well-read minds (Strauss's included). Octavian as the bearer of a silver rose for his cousin's bride-to-be originated in the papal custom of presenting a golden rose to the daughters of the nobility. Only when the third act neared completion did the opera's title – *Der Rosenkavalier* – reflect the pivotal action of its plot.

Such a treasure-trove of rich reference needed its musical equivalent and when in the spring Hofmannsthal sent Strauss the text of the first act, composition, he was told, flowed as easily as the river Loisach through Garmisch. For the first time Strauss's talent for widely contrasted characterisation could be indulged in a confection of styles verging on pastiche. In the priapic Prelude he exaggerated his orchestral love scenes (in *Don Juan*, *Ein Heldenleben*, *Symphonia Domestica* and *Feuersnot*) with deliberate parody; then he moved seamlessly from the tongue-in-cheek Wagnerisms of Octavian and a Mozart minuet for breakfast, through Viennese operetta and Italian *opera seria* to a closing scene of sudden and sustained seriousness. The orchestra, already manipulated with the greatest of dexterity, was slimmed down to a chamber-music intimacy not so far removed from the *Symphonia Domestica*'s most earnest moments – for a while nothing more than a string sextet and solo woodwind – and the rôle of the Marschallin, now become the mouthpiece for Hofmannsthal's profoundest reflections on *das Gleiternde*, took on a greater significance and inner complexity. She would play a vital rôle in the resolution of the opera, Hofmannsthal decided, as 'the central figure for the public', the figure to 'touch once again the more sublime chords of

Set design by Alfred Roller for Act One, Scene One of *Der Rosenkavalier* in Dresden, 1911.

tenderness'. From the start Strauss gave her all the musical help she needed, but he made sure, too, that Octavian, a rôle for a soprano or a mezzo with an impressively wide range, and Sophie, the lyric soprano, had their own strengths and rewards by way of contrast.

'That certain Viennese sentimentality of the parting scene has come off well', Strauss wrote on 22 May 1909, having set the whole act in rough sketch a mere three weeks after he had received it. With an eye on the Alpine weather which was to dictate the pattern of his composition for years to come, he roundly declared that he would finish Act 2 by the end of the summer and Act 3 the next. He knew how full his conducting schedule would be back in Berlin, where, after the sabbatical, he had renewed his contract for another ten years, but nevertheless the estimate was an accurate one.

'Do try and think of an old-fashioned Viennese waltz, sweet and yet saucy, which must pervade the whole of the last act', Hofmannsthal had suggested in April. Strauss, not stopping to wonder whether his poet had forgotten the eighteenth century setting, took the hint and the liberty of spicing the whole score with an abundance of 3/4 time (in the manner of his Austrian namesake whose music he so admired); but he reserved his master-waltz for Baron Ochs in Act 2, using it with innate theatrical skill to bring down the curtain. 'A first class hit', he predicted, and of course he was right. That summer he dictated a revision of Hoffmannsthal's dramatic structure for this act. With the sureness that had prompted greater emphasis on Elektra's recognition scene, he told his librettist that the presentation of the rose and Ochs's coarse badinage up to the second Sophie-Octavian duet were excellent, but that the act then needed to build to a grand climax and burlesque ensemble and subside to a quiet but effective close. 'Believe me: my instinct does not deceive me', he wrote with typical candour. Like Verdi, creator of the operatic figure on whom Ochs was so evidently modelled, he knew what would hold an audience; and the lessons of *Falstaff* must have contributed to his understanding of the politics of construction. Hofmannsthal blustered and pontificated, but ended with a grateful acknowledgment: 'From this one occasion I have learned something fundamental about dramatic work for music which I shall not forget.' Strauss would continually step in to preach many a tactful sermon to his unworldly collaborator in future.

Strauss's dramatic instinct also told him that if the first act was 'leisurely and full of sentiment', and the second lively by way of contrast, then the third should continue the action and rise ultimately to greater lyrical heights. When work began on it in

May 1910 (and Hofmannsthal was only just in time to meet his partner's established schedule), Strauss had once again to insist where the emotional emphasis should fall: he sent back the draft asking for much more in the final scene. The spell should be left to the notes: '. . . it is at the conclusion that a musician, if he has any ideas at all, can achieve his best and supreme effects – so you may safely leave this for me to judge.' The results, penned that summer at white heat once Hofmannsthal had obliged with the extra lines, did not fall short of the promise. Strauss knew that the burlesque earlier in the act culminated in the weakest passages in *Der Rosenkavalier*; but he was in no doubt that the closing trio and duet were the incandescent crowning glory of the opera.

After the inspired plain-sailing of composition, performance problems loomed large that winter, but Strauss was insistent on the very highest standards in every department. He chose Dresden and Schuch once more for the first performance, and a team of singers who, where possible, were consummate actors (by no means a standard prerequisite of the time); he insisted on the celebrated Alfred Roller from the Vienna State Opera as his designer – and his production book became a work of art independent of the opera; and he even managed to enlist the assistance of Max Reinhardt from Berlin, smuggled in uncredited (and much to the understandable chagrin of the producer, Georg

Minnie Nast as Sophie, Carl Perron as a wounded Baron Ochs, and Karl Scheidemantel (right) as Faninal, in the Dresden première of *Der Rosenkavalier*.

Poster announcing the first performance of *Der Rosenkavalier* in Dresden, 26 January 1911.

Toller) towards the end of rehearsals to lend much-needed advice on dramatic realism.

Neither the weakest member of the cast – the tall, thin figure of Carl Perron as Ochs (Richard Mayr, the first choice, could not be released from his contract in Vienna) – nor the ubiquitous intervention of the censor to quibble over some of the Baron's lascivious remarks, could mute the excitement of the first night on 26 January 1911. All 50 performances at Dresden within the year were sold out, and it was the same in Vienna and Milan – even though the Italians, mortified to hear waltzes in an opera, roundly booed the second act. Every time there was the sense of occasion; there still is today, and there always will be if Hofmannsthal's stage directions, which read with all the imaginative detail of a fine novel, are followed to the letter. Yet however opulent the production, it is rare for an audience to leave untouched by the bitter-sweet warnings of the silver rose chords, or the ominous striking of the glockenspiel in the gloom as the Marschallin feels time slip through her fingers. *Der Rosenkavalier* has as much to say about the frailty of the human condition as any of those 'comedies for music' by Mozart to which it pays its individual tribute; and like them it manages to stay light of hand and light of heart as it does so.

A rare photograph of great men together, taken on the set for *Der Rosenkavalier*, 1911. Max Reinhardt, Hofmannsthal and Roller are in the centre of the group standing behind Strauss; on his left is the conductor Ernst von Schuch, on his right the intendant of the Dresden Opera, Count von Seebach.

Eva von der Osten, the first
Octavian in *Der Rosenkavalier*.

The presentation of the rose
in the 1911 production:
Minnie Nast (Sophie), Eva
von der Osten (Octavian).

Chapter 9

The Two Ariadnes

To a generation brought up in the midst of Edwardian comfort, *Der Rosenkavalier* came, with hindsight, to stand as an exuberant requiem for a vanished age. Intending to recreate in a fresh fashion the manners of the time of Mozart and Molière, Strauss had once again marked the mood of his own era, a mood which sensed the sand trickling through the hour-glass. Yet the clocks in Garmisch hardly slowed down or stopped, as a neat rise-and-fall theory of some historians would have us believe. Instead, they began to keep a time of their own. In his next two major projects, Strauss swam vigorously against the general tide to serve his own need for contrasts.

Although when he came to write *Ariadne auf Naxos* Strauss spontaneously predicted the substitution of chamber ensembles for the vast post-Romantic orchestra that became a near-necessity

Strauss at the Berlin première of *Der Rosenkavalier* with Lola Artot de Padilla, his ideal Octavian, and Frieda Hempel as the Marschallin.

One of the few photographs
of Strauss and Hofmannsthal
together, at the poet's home
in Rodaun.

in the austere and unstable climate after the shattering events of
the First World War, in *Die Frau ohne Schatten* he returned to an
epic scale; and small wonder that the changed circumstances after
the war could not, or would not, support this massively-scored
myth of interaction and unity. Both the complicated, overlapping
geneses of these operas and the oscillating moods within them
suggest that the battle between small and large scale, ironic and
heroic, Mozart and Wagner, continued to rage for Strauss, while
the world to which he was largely indifferent made up its mind. If
the Great War could not affect him except when it troubled his
personal circumstances (and in several instances it did, deeply),
then he suffered his own creative crises in the quest to do
something new. The exception among his works of this period,
the ballet *Josephslegende*, shows a genius functioning as a talent
while nothing better could spur his imagination.

The germ of both operas came just after the première of
Rosenkavalier. Strauss, stirred by a Berlin production of *Aida*,
had decided that the time was right for lavish spectacle, and once

more suggested *Semiramis* to Hofmannsthal. Out of the question, came the reply: but Hofmannsthal did ask what Strauss thought of a symbolical fairy-tale with romantic overtones – *Das steinerne Herz*. This set Strauss's fancies running on overtly spectacular elements in the tale and Hofmannsthal had to correct him: the situation was to be simple, its tension a fundamental one between 'the heart that's frozen and the heart that beats'. But *Das steinerne Herz* also fell out of the reckoning and Hofmannsthal instead suggested the idea which was to become the starting point for *Die Frau ohne Schatten*. His letter of 20 March 1911 – which contained as if in passing the outlines of a half-hour chamber opera, *Ariadne auf Naxos* – divulged little about his 'magic fairy tale' save the cunning bait of a female character with many of Pauline's traits, the promise of spectacle and the hint that it would stand in relation to *Die Zauberflöte* as *Der Rosenkavalier* had to *Figaro*.

In fact the larger project was temporarily suspended, though Strauss was highly encouraging. Hofmannsthal always waited like a hopeful receptacle of inspiration for his subject-matter to arrive and he pointed out that if, as he believed, this new work was to be their joint masterpiece, it needed an 'effortless symbolism' which he so far lacked. For Strauss time was pressing; he needed his summer labours cut out for him and all he had before him at the moment was a symphony which, he said, amused him 'less than chasing maybugs'. (This work was to take shape three years later as *Eine Alpensinfonie*, during another of Hofmannsthal's creative blanks.) Meanwhile, Hofmannsthal began work on an adaptation of Molière's *Le Bourgeois Gentilhomme*, though another opera was taking shape in his mind. He told Strauss he conceived it as 'a combination of heroic mythological figures in eighteenth century costume with hooped skirts and ostrich feathers and . . . characters from the *commedia dell'arte*; harlequins and scaramouches representing the *buffo* element which is throughout interwoven with the heroic'. Then came the idea for a wholly new form of entertainment: Hofmannsthal suggested placing the opera as a *divertissement* within his adaptation of Molière's play.

For the play, which left very little Molière once Hofmannsthal had cut five acts down to two and added scenes of his own, Strauss was to supply a succession of incidental dances and songs. He immediately set about writing pastiches of the kind of music Lully had written in his 1670 comedy-ballet collaboration with Molière on the same subject, working in some of the *Cythère* sketches, and though he spent little time on these numbers, they turned out to be delightfully spontaneous and attractive miniatures. Beecham classed them alongside Grieg's *Peer Gynt* pieces and Bizet's contributions to *L'Arlésienne* as supreme examples of incidental music at its most effective. Six of them were to find their way into the *Bürger als Edelmann* (*Bourgeois Gentilhomme*) suite that Strauss compiled in 1917, aptly culminating in the tasty morsels and wry quotations (from Meyerbeer, Wagner, Verdi and his own works) he had liberally laid on for the play's dinner scene.

Strauss, however, was less enthusiastic about Hofmannsthal's operatic scheme, which by now centred on the Ariadne myth. The story could compel his Dionysian spirits and the concept of Mozartian set numbers again certainly appealed, but he realised that so much would depend on the poetry, and his wide knowledge of the classics told him that the heroic posturings integral to such a tale usually led to the most frigid rhetoric. Hofmannsthal, in fact, intended to use the *buffo* element in the work as the necessary counterweight to this, though he had not bargained for Strauss's conception of Zerbinetta, the Columbine character in the Harlequinade, as a coloratura soprano. As if by way of violent reaction, he began to manipulate his Ariadne, intended as a richly human figure and sister to the Marschallin, as the lofty antithesis of her frivolous counterpart. As the project swelled to alarming proportions, the contrast threatened to become schematic: Ariadne became the constant woman, faithful

Set and costume designs by Ernst Stern for the 1912 première of *Ariadne auf Naxos*.

91

unto death, and Zerbinetta, with her stream of love affairs, her all-too-frail opponent. The meeting of Bacchus and Ariadne took on shades of Hofmannsthal's favourite dramatic device of *allomatisches* (mutual transformation), as a transfiguring experience for both the god and the deserted princess.

Hofmannsthal would often insinuate that his intellectual agility left his down-to-earth collaborator bewildered, and there are plenty of commentators to take that opinion as fact. Yet their extensive correspondence on the subject of *Ariadne*, for all Hofmannsthal's high-flown eloquence and Strauss's customary terseness, tells a different story. Strauss seems to have grasped his librettist's implications at every turn but wondered, quite rightly, whether an audience would do the same. *Ariadne auf Naxos* was the first of their joint works where Strauss questioned the dramatic clarity of a newly emerging symbolism. Hofmannsthal's elucidation of the final text is most often quoted, but Strauss's reply on 19 July deserves prominence:

. . . the piece did not fully convince me until after I had read your letter, which is so beautiful and explains the meaning of the action so wonderfully that a superficial musician like myself could not, of course, have tumbled to it. But isn't this a little dangerous? And isn't some of the interpretation still lacking in the action itself? Surely, the symbolism must leap out alive from the action, instead of being dug out of it by subsequent laborious elaboration.

For Strauss, Ariadne and Bacchus never really came alive. Though he built into the final scene a steady crescendo towards the ecstasy of their union, and decked it in the most iridescent textures of which his 38-piece orchestra was capable, he could not quite lend to their themes the 'higher significance' that Hofmannsthal hoped for. What stirred his enthusiasm were Zerbinetta's vagaries, a far more interesting embodiment of the human condition even if the outward form of her *scena* was a virtuoso aria and rondo. In a curious way it was she, rather than the enduring heroine, who for Strauss rekindled the spark of the Marschallin's attitude to life. The ironic intrusion of the clowns, followed by Monsieur Jourdain – *le bourgeois gentilhomme* – was for him a more satisfactory resolution than the lovers' happy end.

The completed entertainment had been intended from the first for Max Reinhardt's Berlin company, but its combined forces of actors, singers and orchestra could not be accommodated within their small theatre. The answer was to transport the entire company to Stuttgart. Once again Strauss the perfectionist and court conductor rode roughshod over the feelings of the Stuttgart actors. Although they were to give most of the performances, they were expected to yield the glamorous first night to the Berliners,

Max Reinhardt in 1935.

and Strauss expressed naïve surprise when the dress rehearsal turned into a fiasco. Nor did Strauss's conducting and a fine cast of singers, which included Maria Jeritza as Ariadne (the first of her unforgettable performances in Strauss's operas), save the opera from the dismay of the theatre-goers in the audience when the première finally took place on 25 October 1912. Hofmannsthal's dramatic link between *Der Bürger als Edelmann* (*Le Bourgeois Gentilhomme*) and *Ariadne* was jettisoned since the evening would otherwise have been too long, and by a splendid irony the opera had to wait while the King of Württemberg presided over an interminable reception following the play.

Hofmannsthal was aware that this 'pretty hybrid', as Strauss called it, could not take root under such circumstances; but he was determined not to let it wither. Perhaps the opera could work better prefaced by a *Vorspiel* (a prelude) set mostly to *secco* recitative, instead of the spoken prologue he had written; perhaps this *Vorspiel* could even be fashioned from a backstage scene Hofmannsthal had already written for *Der Bürger als Edelmann*. Strauss, now at work on *Die Frau ohne Schatten*, replied that it was better to let *Ariadne* alone. He told Hofmannsthal on 15 June 1913 that the proposed text for the *Vorspiel* was not at all to his liking, as it necessitated the portrayal of a composer, something that was distasteful to him. Possibly he felt quite simply that he had to establish fresh perspectives before he could take up the thread of *Ariadne* once more. But by 1916, when Hofmannsthal's inspiration for *Die Frau ohne Schatten* had dried up (and for the sake of clarity it is perhaps wiser to refer to that opera's progress in the following chapter), Strauss felt ready to resume the *Vorspiel*. Now the figure of the Composer pleased him better, but his suggestion that the part should be taken by a woman *en travesti* incurred Hofmannsthal's thundering displeasure. Echoes of Octavian apart, it made good practical sense: the principal baritones would not accept such a small rôle, however crucial, and the tenors were terrible. Paradoxically, a convincing female actress-singer would make a more realistic impression. Strauss's clear-sighted opinion on the music of the *Vorspiel*, completed towards the end of May 1916, needs no further corroboration:

The scene between Zerbinetta and the Composer has really come out very delightfully; it is one of my very best ideas. The whole thing is, in my opinion, rather well organised and climaxed, and should be successful in its own right, without the opera proper.

The *Vorspiel* is a procession of deft character sketches with each figure owning a recognisable set of musical gestures, set in the *parlando* style of parts of *Rosenkavalier* and culminating, like that opera's first act, in a sustained single scene. This and the original opera, shorn of its ironic ending and some passages in the Harlequinade and Zerbinetta's aria, constitute the form in which we know *Ariadne auf Naxos* best today. The first performance at the Vienna State Opera on 4 October 1916, conducted by Franz Schalk, included a Composer who fulfilled all of Strauss's hopes for that rôle (and others to come) – the great Lotte Lehmann. The new generation of Strauss sopranos was beginning to take shape.

This was not the last of the Molière entertainment, however. When Hofmannsthal came to revise his stage adaptation of *Le Bourgeois Gentilhomme* (*Der Bürger als Edelmann*) in 1917, adding entire scenes which included the reinstatement of Molière's delightfully preposterous mammamouche ceremony, he needed

Lotte Lehmann as the Composer in the 1916 version of *Ariadne auf Naxos*, Vienna.

more incidental music from Strauss. The two men now came closest to a rift, springing from an apparently trivial disagreement. Strauss decided the Act 1 curtain needed music to gain its full impact, and persisted in his belief. Hofmannsthal could pontificate as much as he pleased, asserting his 'superior taste' and setting forth any number of arguments, but throughout the summer months Strauss remained firm. The pattern, as always, was completed with the playwright's grateful acknowledgement that the other was right. In terms of the achievement, it seems of small importance. Strauss acquitted himself with solid craftsmanship, and in another group of numbers he opulently refashioned some of Lully's dance movements from the 1670 *Bourgeois Gentilhomme* ballet. Two of these and the wholly original *courante* joined the extant movements in his *Bürger als Edelmann* suite.

Out of the three Molière 'versions', Beecham preferred the first – perhaps because that was the one he had introduced to London in 1913 and then, at least, with the splendid Henry Tree as Jourdain, it had certainly worked. He felt that the *Vorspiel* smacked of commerce and he revived the original entertainment several times with great success. Those of us who have not had the chance to judge for ourselves would not easily forego the memorable characterisations of 1916 – the Composer with his adolescent glooms and raptures, the Prima Donna's glittering gestures, the Dancing Master's pirouette. Nor would we want to miss the sharpened medium of caricature in which the chamber orchestra is so deftly employed. It had its birth in *Till Eulenspiegel*, and in *Der Rosenkavalier* Strauss hinted that it might have much to say in an operatic context. But here, for the first time, it found something like equal prominence as a characterising agent alongside the vocal lines. Strauss was convinced, after completing the *Vorspiel*, that his real talent was as the great operetta composer of the century. But then he still had the vital conclusion of *Die Frau ohne Schatten* to write.

Chapter 10

A War Casualty

For Strauss the outbreak of the First World War in the summer of 1914 meant at first only a sad decline in artistic standards: salaries at the Berlin Court Theatre were reduced, the Meiningen players found themselves out of work and the Opera House in Frankfurt put on a season of standard repertory. When the terrible actualities of warfare became apparent, he had a measure of cynicism about the patriotic campaign and his share of concern for the victims. 'It is sickening . . . to read how Young Germany is to emerge cleansed and purified from this "glorious war"', he wrote to Hofmannsthal in February 1915, 'when in fact one must be thankful if the poor blighters are at least cleansed of their lice and bed-bugs and cured of their infections and once more weaned from murder!' He felt that one should leave politics to the politicians and immerse oneself in the projects to hand: 'only hard work can console us; only hard work can bring us victory'.

He was personally affected by the war in three ways. First, his savings, lodged with the banker Sir Edgar Speyer in London, were confiscated; he recalled that he fell into a profound depression for a week and then started afresh as if nothing had happened. Then, he and Pauline were fretting over their son reaching the age when he could be compulsorily enlisted in the army. Their anxiety came to an end in 1918 when Franz was considered medically unfit for service. But perhaps unhappiest of all, the sensitive Hofmannsthal was profoundly affected by the international madness of the times and his inability to meet the deadline for the third act of *Die Frau ohne Schatten* struck at Strauss's creative flow. It was surely this, and not any blank incomprehension of the densely wrought tale on Strauss's part, which left the fairy-tale opera a palpable casualty of circumstance after the successes which preceded it.

That 'effortless symbolism' posited by Hofmannsthal for *Die Frau ohne Schatten* in his letter to Strauss of 1911 finally started to take on a more definite shape two years later, when the first version of *Ariadne* was complete. By then the enthusiasm of the two collaborators was as great as it had been at the time of *Der Rosenkavalier*. From Hofmannsthal's notebooks it is evident that

Hofmannsthal and Strauss: silhouette by Bithorn, 1914.

the fundamental themes of *Die Frau ohne Schatten* were already clear in his mind when he wrote that seminal letter. In the midst of his mighty synthesis, combining elements from Eastern mythologies with European legend and a Viennese folk play, the basic scheme remained constant. This was a drama exploring the tensions between two couples, a fairy pair and a mortal pair of *Singspiel* tradition, and the *donnée* was the fairy empress's desire for the mortal woman's child. This hint of *Die Zauberflöte* became crucial in the evolving plan.

In 1912 Hofmannsthal wrote an introduction to a volume of Goethe's stage works. Among them was a sequel to the Mozart opera in which Goethe extends the trials of Pamina and Tamino and Papageno and Papagena by sending them on a quest for children to enrich their marriages, and in the fresh impetus of ideas at the beginning of 1913, Hofmannsthal explained to Strauss how in the similar theme of their opera the transformation would be achieved by the mutual reactions of the couples to each other:

There are eleven significant, almost pantomimically incisive situations but it is their combination – in which two worlds, two pairs of beings, two interwoven conflicts take their turn, reflect each other and eventually find their equilibrium – which gives unity to the whole work.

98

Even seen merely as a spectacle it would be most remarkable and attractive; through the music it will receive its final consummation, through the music which will merge both worlds, will reflect the one in the other, will indeed transform one in to the other, as an alchemist transmutes the elements.

Central would be the redemptive figure of the Empress, the shadowless woman of the title, who would be tempted by the Mephistophelian nurse to take the mortal woman's shadow (symbolically, her sign of fertility at one level and in a wider sense the expression of her complete personality), because her year-long union with the earthbound Emperor had failed to give her one of her own. But, finally, she would come to realise, through the goodness of the other woman's husband, that she could not buy her own happiness at the cost of another person's suffering. The 'transmutation' Hofmannsthal mentioned would make the fairy pair more human, the humans more imaginative.

In March 1913 Strauss and Hofmannsthal were able to let the plan take further shape on a motoring tour of Italy. They had met on occasions before, but this opportunity for discussion and direct collaboration was one they both felt essential to a mutual understanding of their most complex joint work so far. Strauss, as usual, was inspired by the clear Italian skies and the sunshine. One night he conceived the idea of chamber forces for the spirit world and full orchestra for the earthlings. He did not in the end adhere to it, but in the first act he came close to an appropriate use of contrasts in the control of his huge orchestra. It was enough to unleash, in startling turn, the teeming multitude of moods in the act – ethereal and transparent for the Empress, sinister for the Nurse, naïvely romantic for the Emperor, violent, simple and serene for the dyer, Barak, and his wife. There were more shades of Wagner than in any of his works since *Guntram*; but this, too, was apt since Hofmannsthal's extensive reading of Wagner's librettos had infused inescapable parallels in situation with the *Ring* and, in the beautiful quiet curtain to the act, to *Die Meistersinger*. Only, perhaps, in *Don Quixote* had Strauss woven so many diverse strains into his sound world.

The first act, however, was not completed until the following June. Before he could give full attention to the opera, Strauss had composed the massive *Festliches Präludium* for the opening of the Vienna Konzerthaus in October 1913 and the sumptuously harmonised *Deutsche Motette*, to a text by Rückert, for the chorus of the Berlin Court Opera. This most difficult of choral works, divided into 16 parts with the addition of four solo lines, is a typical extension, in choral context, of Strauss's near-impossible demands on the compasses of his orchestral players. In style, it

Leonid Massine as Joseph in
Josephslegende.

remained only a small advance on the *Zwei Gesänge* ('Der Abend'
and 'Hymne'), supreme examples of Strauss's mastery of choral
writing both in the glowing progressions of block chords and the
clarity of the polyphony.

There was also tiresome work to be despatched that summer:
music for a ballet for Diaghilev, *Josephslegende*, to a book by
Hofmannsthal and Count Harry Kessler. Strauss had adored the
lavish opulence of Diaghilev's already legendary Ballets Russes
when they came to Berlin during the 1912-13 season, and he was

honoured by Diaghilev's commission for him to make his own contribution. But he soon found that biblical 'good-boy Joseph' interested him as a character even less than Jokanaan, and Hofmannsthal's high-mindedness over the spiritual revelations of God's beloved could only have stirred his malicious obstinacy still further. His equal loss to find anything striking for the sensual provocations of Potiphar's wife was the result of an unwillingness to repeat himself. *Salome* had exhausted all there was to say on the subject, and it is strange to find Hofmannsthal, who in other circumstances seems to have realised that his colleague's need to inhabit a new world with every fresh project was as great as his own, prompting resuscitation of old themes.

When the production was premièred in Paris on 14 May 1914, everything that might earlier have inspired Strauss – designs by Bakst after Veronese (one of Strauss's favourite artists), choreography by Fokine and the whiff of a scandal in the offing – went towards wrapping up this glutinous, routine score. Leonid Massine as Joseph, a highly acceptable substitute for Nijinsky (whose rift with Diaghilev had led to his absence), carried off the occasion, though few were fooled by the music, for all its dazzling surface. Only George Bernard Shaw, irritated again by Ernest Newman, held Strauss's contribution, when he saw the ballet in London later that year, to be 'a magnificent piece of work'. This time it was Newman, describing Strauss's style as 'the self-satisfied, platitudinous orotundity of the leading article and party speech', whom posterity has proved right; though he was wise to caution that 'whether he [Strauss] has written himself out for good or only for the moment remains to be seen'.

Had Newman been privy to the Garmisch workshop, he might have been still more wary of risking prophecy. In the summer of 1914 Strauss was busy with the second act of *Die Frau ohne Schatten*. He had some problems where he least expected them – with the Pauline-like character of Barak's discontented wife, but there are no hints, in the correspondence or the music, that he fell behind his librettist in understanding exactly what was needed. Even Hofmannsthal's extra layers of symbolism could be understood simply as accessories to the enchanted medium of the fairy-tale. The steadily mounting tension of the act through its five diverse scenes – the music inevitably taking on a Wagnerian density as supernatural forces overwhelm the characters – reflects perfectly in its nightmarish interweaving of themes what Hofmannsthal referred to as 'the polyphonic interaction of the couples'. The customary abundance of cuts exercised by conductors in this act only makes it seem longer, a paradox of which Strauss seems to have been fully conscious. Given a firm hand, clear direction and a soprano capable of handling the vocal

Set design by Alfred Roller for the Vienna première of *Die Frau ohne Schatten*, 1919. Act Two: the Falcon House.

demands on Barak's wife in this act, its impact will not go amiss.

Hofmannsthal completed his rough draft of Act 3 two weeks before the Serbian ultimatum, which followed so swiftly on the heels of the Sarajevo assassination and led to the start of the First World War. Almost immediately he was drummed into the army, and the vital meeting he wanted with Strauss to discuss the opera's hard-won resolution and to hear the first two acts in piano score could no longer be held. The following March, nearing the time when the composer would need to begin the next part of his schedule, Hofmannsthal was deeply depressed and tired. Strauss lacked true sympathy and understanding . . . 'am fresh and rested and full of energy. Why are you letting your spirits droop like this? You may depend on Germany', he rallied. When the manuscript was finally in his hands a month later, he encountered the same problems he had met in the rhetoric of Bacchus and Ariadne. He understood the substance well enough, but receptive friends did not. What he had was still a mere sketch which needed life and soul. But soon Hofmannsthal provided the necessary amendment and some extra lines for the opening scene between Barak and his wife, and the first scene proceeded at a fine sweep.

102

Strauss now urgently needed the rest: the Empress's decision in the temple not to take the shadow was as significant a moment in the opera's structure as the recognition scene in *Elektra*. 'The success of the whole thing depends on this moment', Strauss urged. Hofmannsthal was serving in a diplomatic post in Poland, uninspired and out of sorts. By the time his revised draft reached Garmisch, delayed by postal vagaries, it was October and Strauss's winter hibernation was due.

Strauss had, however, used the previous winter following the outbreak of war to complete his 1911 'left-handed' project, *Eine Alpensinfonie*. It was his first purely orchestral work since the *Symphonia Domestica* of 1903, and the first since *Aus Italien* to record his sensations of the natural world. Now that he had mastered character study in operatic form, it was time to do something new with the symphonic poem. Perhaps the death of Mahler, on 18 May 1911, had been a shaping influence; but when he came to complete his 'symphony', Strauss solved his attitude to nature worship in quite a different way. He stretched his graphic powers to the limit in depicting a waterfall, an alpine meadow, the strip-cartoon manoeuvres of a struggling mountaineer (remembered from a teenage climbing expedition in the Bavarian Alps) and a storm; but around these episodes he used a large orchestra to weave rich, fatly scored lyric rhapsodies at greater length than any he had written before. The work is no more a conventional four movement symphony than Sibelius's final essay in the genre. Strauss bound its 21 sections masterfully within a huge symphonic arch, which reaches its peak at the mountain-top, as the subject dictates, and runs the rest of its course in an almost contrary manner, continually developing its themes as it goes. The return journey, dominated by the expectation and onset of the storm, contains some ideas akin in their strangeness and mood of awesome anticipation to the gathering darkness in the second act of *Die Frau ohne Schatten*, just completed; but the characteristically poignant epilogue fails to run the course of its predecessors. Steadily the composer steers us back into the B flat minor gloom of the opening bars, the mountain theme casts its final Wagnerian shadow and the strings begin their usually confident walking tune listlessly, again in the minor, only to die before they can complete it. Could there have been a more timely or disconcerting farewell to the splendours of the pre-war years, or a surer mirror of the distress which Strauss refused to allow any lasting hold over him?

Eine Alpensinfonie received its first performance on 28 October 1915 in Berlin. The orchestra Strauss conducted on this occasion was that of the Dresden Court Opera, to whom the work was a grateful present for all the operatic successes he had so far enjoyed in that city. *Die Frau ohne Schatten*, meanwhile, waited ominously in the wings. It needed, by contrast to its orchestral contemporary, a monumental, optimistic conclusion which came to seem more facile the longer the war lasted. Paeans to the resolution of human struggle had come uneasily even to Wagner, who had surely been happier in the inconclusive end of *Götterdämmerung* than in the harp-spangled benediction of *Parsifal*; how much harder they were for Strauss, with his love of complex human nature and his suspicion of the mystical or the sublime. Yet perhaps – and it is a big 'perhaps' – he might have had the strength of will to solve the problem successfully in his own unique manner. What really sealed the fate of the whole venture was that by the following spring of 1916 when he still lacked the improved text from Hofmannsthal, Strauss turned to the *Ariadne* Prologue (*Vorspiel*) and found on successfully completing it that it had blocked out the high confidence needed for *Die Frau*. He wrote to Hofmannsthal that June:

When you've heard the new *Vorspiel* . . . you'll realise that I have a definite talent for operetta. And since my tragic vein is more or less exhausted, and since tragedy in the theatre, after this war, strikes me as something rather idiotic and childish, I should like to apply this irrepressible talent of mine – after all, I'm the only composer nowadays with some real humour and sense of fun and a marked gift for parody. Indeed, I feel downright called upon to become the Offenbach of the twentieth century . . .

When he was finally able to start on the temple and final scenes later that summer, he knew that the conclusion, 'massive and artificial' as he later called it, lacked the breath of life:

Characters like the Emperor and Empress, and also the Nurse, can't be filled with red corpuscles in the same way as a Marschallin, an Octavian, or an Ochs. No matter how I rack my brain – and I'm toiling really hard, sifting and sifting – my heart's only half in it, and once the head has to do the major part of the work you get a breath of academic chill (which my wife rightly calls 'note-spinning') which no bellows can ever kindle in to a real fire.

All the same, his attitude must be seen in the context of that time and the markedly new atmosphere of the *Ariadne* Prologue. Caught in the same breath of inspiration which had so magically captured the Empress's awakening in Act 1 or the Emperor's strange and sombre soliloquy outside the falcon-house in Act 2 – a new vein succeeding where the Ariadne-Bacchus duet had faltered – his response might have been different. But he worked scrupulously enough for the illusion of the theatre to take over at the end in performance, as Hofmannsthal later observed. The

Pre-war Berlin: *Unter den Linden*, circa 1910.

creators, however, had to wait a year before they could see for themselves. The war had still not run its course when the score was completed in February 1918. Such a backdrop conflicted with the romantic nature of the opera and worked against the kind of production needed to do *Die Frau ohne Schatten* justice.

Chapter 11

Marriage Contracts

As the Great War drew slowly to a close, Strauss sought the kind of change and refuge in his conducting career that he had already found in his private life through the Garmisch villa. He had been in Berlin for nearly two decades; he had seen the system of court patronage undermined, royal support withdrawn and financial restrictions imposed. His 'art-egotism', as one colleague was to call it, saw no reason why the great musical establishments should be affected by external affairs. Yet he now saw the onslaught of post-war austerity posing a very real threat to the great works of a long musical tradition; he felt they needed a fresh and lively lease of life and saw Vienna as the ideal centre for consolidating this kind of hold.

In fact the arts in Berlin flourished in an unexpected and invigorating manner after Strauss left the city to become director of the Vienna State Opera in 1919. The pianist Claudio Arrau, who spent many of his formative years there, has recalled how the 'great misery' of inflation and unemployment, which the Social Democratic government of 1919 could do nothing to assuage, only encouraged people to seek 'a better life in culture'. In such an atmosphere progressive composers with whom Strauss found himself increasingly out of sympathy – Hindemith, Schoenberg, Stravinsky and Bartók (who claimed that his compositional incentive was established as a result of hearing *Also sprach Zarathustra* in 1902) – were welcomed enthusiastically. A new kind of opera reflecting the harsher realities of post-war life was just around the corner and its exponents, Kurt Weill and Berthold Brecht, were making their respective experiments at the beginning of the 1920s.

Strauss's first concert as conductor in Vienna had been with the Berlin Philharmonic Orchestra in 1897; acquaintance with the Vienna Philharmonic began in the 1907-8 season, and when he returned from conducting *Elektra*, *Rosenkavalier* and *Ariadne* at the Vienna Court Opera in April 1918, he announced to Hofmannsthal his hopes of gaining a foothold there once the current director, Hans Gregor, had left (which then seemed likely). In the following month he withdrew from his commitments at the Berlin Court

Strauss and Franz Schalk, his co-director at the Vienna State Opera, before the 1919 première of *Die Frau ohne Schatten*.

Opera after a quarrel with the autocratic Intendant, Georg von Hülsen, although he did temporarily stand in as director of the new Berlin State Opera for a further year and continued conducting Staatskapelle concerts until 1920. The rest of the summer, as usual, was given over to composing, and by the winter months Strauss began to formulate an artistic policy for Vienna of a type that had been impossible in Berlin or for that matter in any of his youthful conducting posts. He proposed a division of labour similar to that put forward by his most illustrious predecessor in Vienna, Mahler, and allayed Hofmannsthal's concern that he would lavish too much attention on his own works by replying that Berlin was one thing, Vienna quite another.

For once, Strauss's confidence proved unrealistic in several respects. Negotiations he and Hofmannsthal conducted on separate occasions with the new Vienna Intendant, Leopold von Andrian-Werburg, led only to the offer of a joint directorship with Franz Schalk, a staff conductor in Mahler's heyday and the man responsible for the musical supervision of the Vienna premières of *Rosenkavalier* and the 1916 *Ariadne*. It was obvious from the first, however, that Strauss would reign supreme and leave the long-serving Schalk a great deal of hard work during his lengthy absences. Then the collapse of the Austrian monarchy resulted in the Court Opera coming under state control in 1919, shortly before Strauss's contract was announced on 1 March. This augured greater financial restraints than he had anticipated. The staff of the Opera, moreover, were set against the composer-as-director, and those who signed a petition to obstruct his appointment (there were some 800 signatures) expressed Hofmannsthal's initial reservations over the creation of an arena for the display of Strauss operas. Their deepest fears, however, were that the change would mean older and established 'stars' being superseded by others who pleased the new director better. In the end, the counterforce of the Viennese intelligentsia, offering welcome, proved stronger. Agreement was reached for Strauss to take up his new post at the beginning of December.

Before he did so, he was finally able to see *Die Frau ohne Schatten* reach the Vienna stage on 10 October. If this was an inauguration which added fuel to the company's ostensible grievances, its authentic Viennese cast must have gone some way to setting their minds at rest. There was Maria Jeritza, the ideal choice for the pivotal rôle of the Empress; there (on hand this time after having been unavailable for the Dresden *Rosenkavalier*) was Richard Mayr as Barak; there too were Lotte Lehmann and the established tenor Karl Aagard-Oestvig as the Emperor. Schalk was the conductor and Roller returned as designer, since once again only the best would suffice for the visual spectacle of the fairy tale. Yet it was not a success. The sets proved cumbersome in the many scene-changes and reports suggest that players and singers were under-rehearsed. Nor was Vienna, suffering the extremes of post-war privation, in the mood for this kind of work. It fared better in Dresden, though subsequent performances in Germany's numerous smaller opera houses proved inadequate, as composer and librettist had predicted. Not until 1977 did Karl Böhm's production in Vienna provide a beacon for others by assembling the kind of cast needed to ensure the opera's continuance.

Lotte Lehmann had spent part of the summer of 1919 being coached for her rôle in *Die Frau ohne Schatten* by Strauss at his Garmisch retreat. Though she had no notion then, her sympathetic observation of the marital relations between Richard and Pauline was preparing her for a later Strauss rôle – the wife in *Intermezzo*. Pauline, once the anxious bride of the young musician, had over the years acquired a certain notoriety for her sharp tongue and fiery temper, her presence at rehearsals and performances nervously anticipated by the interpreters of her husband's works. At home she exaggerated the virtues of the

The Strauss Family: Richard and Pauline with their son in Berlin, early 1900s.

German *Hausfrau* to a degree which verged on the obsessive: visitors had to wipe their feet on three doormats before entering, and the floors were clean enough to dine from. There were plenty of witnesses like Alma Mahler to dwell on the vituperative side of Pauline's nature and to take her often scathing criticisms of her husband's work at face value. Strauss made no effort to disabuse acquaintances of his wife's nervous temperament, accepting it with wry indifference and imperturbable good nature. 'The whole world's admiration interests me less than one of Pauline's tantrums', he told Lotte Lehmann. Only in private circumstances did the more tender, loving side of Pauline's character, already advertised along with the obverse in *Ein Heldenleben* and

Strauss and Pauline in the 1930s with their elder grandson Richard in Vienna.

Symphonia Domestica, become apparent. Lehmann was one of the few who noticed it, or who took the trouble to say so with typical understanding. Strauss would often accompany Pauline in evening *Lieder* recitals at Garmisch, and Lehmann refers to them here:

I often caught a glance or a smile passing between her and her husband, touching in its love and happiness, and I began to sense something of the profound affection between those two human beings, a tie so elemental in its strength that none of Pauline's shrewish truculence could ever trouble it seriously.

Lehmann's was a generous tribute, but Strauss was already at work to surpass it. Again he resolved to set Pauline and himself to music, making quite sure this time, by choosing operatic form, that the message could be clearly understood. Everything the world knew about his wife was there in the text, distilled in neat epigrams; everything he alone knew would be enshrined in the music. Back in 1916, when Strauss made known to Hofmannsthal his attraction towards operetta (in remarks quoted towards the end of the previous chapter), he thought he might employ it either

110

in political satire on the strange new 'types' the war had produced or in 'an extremely modern, absolutely realistic, domestic and character comedy'. Hofmannsthal derided what he thought was a vulgar idea, but the playwright Hermann Bahr (one of the Viennese intellectual circle which also embraced Artur Schnitzler) pointed the way. Intrigued by Bahr's *Das Konzert*, which dealt with the misunderstandings between a musician and his wife, Strauss confided to him an incident in his own married life which he thought might go rather well to music. In the early 1900s, while he was away on tour, a telegram had arrived at the Knesebeckstrasse apartment from a notorious Berlin tart, couching in amorous terms a request to '*Kapellmeister* Richard Strauss' for a couple of theatre tickets. Pauline opened it and without a moment's thought instigated divorce proceedings. Only after frantic investigation did Strauss solve the riddle. The woman who had sent the telegram – one Mitze Mücke – after briefly meeting Josef Stransky, principal conductor in Prague, had brazenly taken up a friend's suggestion that he should get her tickets for the opera. The only Kapellmeister she had found in the Berlin directory was Strauss, so she assumed he was the man in question. The error revealed, a serious crisis was briskly resolved.

Bahr, however, would take no further part in the project when he saw Strauss so much in control of his own material, and he gave him every encouragement to be his own librettist. It was one of the composer's proudest moments when he was told after one performance that his finished text was good enough to stand as a play in its own right. He was justly proud of its dramatic architecture. Pauline's phrases and character formed the backbone of the opera, but they and the anecdote alone would not have been enough. Modern as the cinematic sequence of 14 scenes undoubtedly was (Berg's *Wozzeck* and Shostakovich's *Lady Macbeth of Mtsensk* were still to come), it had to be balanced by traditional values in the development of character. Strauss took four scenes to show Pauline (thinly described as 'Christine'; he became 'Robert Storch') first as the world knew her, cajoling her husband or parading her exalted rank as a Major-General's daughter on a toboggan-run, before casting her in an increasingly sympathetic light as the gullible sponsor of an unscrupulous young Baron (this incident, too, was taken from life). In the scene where she sits by the fireside musing over her absent husband, he plumbed the depths to show her as she really was: here above any of the other portraits is the soul of Pauline glowingly enshrined in an A flat major interlude of surpassing, transparent beauty. Then, with the crisis of the telegram, he soon shifted the focus to the bewildered husband, skat-playing and conducting in Vienna: a parallel movement set in vigorous motion and resolved with

111

merciful swiftness in a reconciliation and duet where the singers at last join together in a simple but melodically effective conclusion. The title eventually chosen for the opera, *Intermezzo*, not only captured the spirit in which it was written but also provided a fascinating reference, intentional or not, to Schnitzler's play of the same name, dealing with a marriage that is anything but perfect.

Hofmannsthal had to admit, when he finally saw *Intermezzo* in 1928, that a trivial subject had been endowed with a greater seriousness than he had expected. At its core this light and witty conversation-piece, taking the chamber-music refinement and instrumental commentary of the *Ariadne* Prologue one stage further, deals with a disturbance that has its links with *Die Frau ohne Schatten*. Both in the second act of that opera and in the interludes framing the Prater scenes of *Intermezzo*, frenzied orchestral writing illustrates the crisis of a placid husband driven to the limits of his endurance by a shrewish but fundamentally loving wife. The operas are very different, but the depth of emotion is comparable, as Strauss pointed out in his reply to Hofmannsthal's congratulations:

The Skat game, Act Two, Scene One of *Intermezzo*, in the Dresden première of 1924. Note the cultivated resemblance of Josef Correck (singing Robert Storch, second from the left) to the composer.

Harmless and insignificant as the incidents which prompted this piece may be, they nevertheless result, when all is said and done, in the most difficult psychological conflicts that can disturb the human heart.

'And this is brought out only by the music', he added. Giving rein to this belief, he had allowed the orchestra in the interludes between the 'realistic' scenes to tell the full story of the characters' deepest feelings. One respected Strauss authority has seen the turbulent polyphony which expresses the husband's despairing bewilderment as absurd, given its kinship to Barak's wrath. The charge of disproportion becomes a virtue if one accepts the obvious equation: Barak and Storch, the husband, suffer the same anguish. By the side of these elaborate sections of the score, the sophisticated delicacy and poise of the domestic scenes support the singers' *parlando* lines tautly, the 50-piece orchestra being used to sparing and telling effect. Strauss's concern over balance and his avowal that every word should be heard as set down in the written introduction to *Intermezzo* proved no mere theory: in a good performance we miss nothing.

Intermezzo, which occupied Strauss intermittently from 1918 through to 1923, received its first performance in Dresden on 4 November 1924. Fritz Busch, Fritz Reiner's successor at Dresden, and best known for the standards he was later to set at Glyndebourne from 1934-39, conducted, and both Lotte Lehmann and Josef Correck were made up to bear a strong resemblance to their characters' real-life counterparts. Even the sets paid strict attention to the Strauss family residence (contemporary Garmisch rather than turn-of-the-century Berlin, since everything should have an absolutely modern flavour). And what did Pauline think of it all? Lotte Lehmann ventured to say to her after the performance what a marvellous tribute her husband had paid her. 'I don't give a damn', she replied, loudly and clearly.

Intermezzo was the only substantial fruit of Strauss's post-war and Vienna years, though they were rich in songs. The cycle *Krämerspiegel* (Shopkeeper's Mirror) of 1918 was a barbed, acid retort to publishers over copyright wrangles, punning on the names of the different firms in a manner remarkably similar to that of Spitzweg, Strauss's first publisher, in a letter to the 20-year-old composer of the Horn Concerto. *Krämerspiegel* also contained in its piano interlude one of Strauss's richest thematic ideas, later to reappear as the Moonlight Music in *Capriccio* (1941). Also from 1918 are the three *Ophelia-Lieder* and the six Brentano settings, the finest inspirations of their kind in the later years. The charge that Strauss had lost his impetus after the war forgets or disdains these works and *Intermezzo*, and rests with the ballet *Schlagobers* (Whipped Cream), performed at the Vienna

State Opera on 9 May 1924. This often ponderous affair with an impossible scenario only tells us, like *Josephslegende*, that for Strauss there was every difference between a work he took on freely and one that acquired the nature of a compulsion. Even so, the *Parergon* (or 'side-work') of 1925, on the child's theme from *Symphonia Domestica*, did not share the spontaneity of the other family-based inspirations. Written as thanksgiving for his son Franz's recovery from the typhus which he had contracted on honeymoon in Egypt, it was also the fulfilment of a promise to the pianist Paul Wittgenstein. Wittgenstein, who had lost an arm serving in the war, showed extraordinary perseverance in his concert career by commissioning a series of works which took into account his disability. Other composers Wittgenstein approached included Prokofiev, Britten and Ravel, whose Concerto for the Left Hand remains the finest and best known of these commissions.

The promises pledged over the Vienna State Opera contract were mostly fulfilled. Strauss's operas remained an essential cornerstone of the repertoire, since he knew their worth and felt it their due; at the same time his painstaking concern over revivals honoured his concern for the operatic tradition. In 1922 he made his views on new works clear by suggesting that the opera houses of Berlin and Vienna did not provide ideal launches for the works of young composers; these would be better sustained within the subscription series of medium-sized theatres (this notion of the old masters' academy and the experimental laboratory was one he held up until his death). All the same, he agreed that Austrian composers had a right to be heard in their national forum and during Strauss's Vienna tenure the first performances of outstanding operas such as Zemlinsky's *Der Zwerg*, Korngold's *Die tote Stadt* and Pfitzner's *Palestrina* saw his guidelines put into practice. The company was in fine form, and it toured Argentina and Brazil for three months in 1920, with Strauss conducting his own operas to resounding acclaim. In 1922 he paid a second visit to North America and London welcomed him back the following year. The young Adrian Boult met him at one of Elgar's lunch parties in St James's Street, answering Elgar's stories with his own in German. In his autobiography Boult describes the conducting style of Strauss at this time:

. . . although Strauss's beat looked rather wooden it was in fact most sympathetic and flexible, and he would give a little time wherever it was needed to avoid a scramble; but so little that the ordinary listener was unaware of any *rubato*.

As a model of economy, Boult rated Strauss at the top of the conducting profession, equal to Artur Nikisch and Felix Weingartner.

But financial conflict was to signal the end of Strauss's tenure in Vienna. Although Strauss never sought more money than he felt absolutely essential to maintain artistic standards, the economic climate had hardly improved and the authorities found his costly manoeuvres untenable. To add to this, Schalk, Strauss's co-director, became dissatisfied with his secondary rôle in Vienna. In 1924 he won the support of the authorities and managed to have a clause inserted in his contract giving him sole responsibility during Strauss's absences. During rehearsals for *Intermezzo* in Dresden, with further controversy over Lotte Lehmann's leave of absence from Vienna to sing the rôle of Christine, Strauss heard about Schalk's action and tendered his resignation. He had no intention of withdrawing his influence entirely: to celebrate his 60th birthday, the authorities had given him a plot of land beside the Belvedere on which to build a house, and contact with Vienna was as essential as his continuing good relations with Berlin if he wanted to ensure the future of his works. He did not, however, have an opera performed at the Vienna State Opera until 1929, when Clemens Krauss took over from Schalk. Krauss had become a trusted and infallible deputy and was one of Strauss's most sympathetic interpreters. (He had conducted the first performance of the ballet for which Strauss had made small-scale arrangements of harpsichord pieces by Couperin, and in 1942 he prompted a sequel from Strauss for a similar entertainment, *Verklungene Feste*, published as the Divertimento.)

Meanwhile, the most important Viennese link, Hofmannsthal, had been racking his tired brain, trying desperately for five years to find a suitable theme for a new operatic collaboration. Strauss was full of promising suggestions culled from his extensive reading, suggesting subjects from Lucian and Plautus or the setting of a down-at-heel Sparta he had read about in Burckhardt. Hofmannsthal's ideas, among them a handling of the Danae myth 'in the French, with German gravity at the core', appeared regularly only to sink back into the past. Even Helen of Troy as a theme seems to have vanished again by 1923. In February a despondent Hofmannsthal apologised:

Pray believe me that it is not indifference or, worse still, lack of inclination which prevents me from getting down to producing a suitable scenario . . . Strangely enough, in the old days a suitable subject used to occur to me so readily – today it is much harder . . . humble and energetic goodwill must, I hope, be rewarded in the long run by the idea.

It was Helen, however, who held Strauss's imagination fast: possibly the promise of another marriage celebration, this time with his old collaborator, had captured his enthusiasm. The manner of extending or altering the ancient conceits of Helen had bold precedents. The Greek poet Stesichorus had devised a neat excuse for Helen's divinity; she had been whisked off, guiltless, by the gods to Egypt while a phantom Helen wreaked havoc on Troy, and Euripides sent up this idea outrageously in his satyr-play *Helen*. Hofmannsthal turned everything on its head by introducing a sorceress, Aithra, who would gull the cuckolded Menelaus into merely believing his artful wife innocent of the events in Troy. In a second act (with a third originally envisaged) the couple would be reconciled through truth alone: honest, realistic means would have to be used as contrast, though Hofmannsthal confessed that he had not thought this through when Strauss enthusiastically began composing the text of the first act in October 1923.

Frequently Hofmannsthal would warn his colleague that a light style was of the essence, but when he gravely announced that 'there is no German artist who does not become more heavy-handed over what he does than he ought to be', he was sounding in this instance his own epitaph. Strauss never had the 'numbers' scheme he wanted from him nor the spoken dialogue and at the beginning of 1924 alarm bells began to ring. 'At the time I started writing, I did not yet realise how much the second act was to step up on to a higher lyrical plane', Hofmannsthal announced. Strauss began to fret over the complications of the couple's new trials, now embroidered with a lovesick Arab chieftain and his son, hyper-Tristanish magic potions and a final apotheosis of sacred marriage in the 'massive and artificial style' of *Die Frau ohne Schatten*. He must have been further struck by a letter from Rolland, who had seen *Ariadne* for the first time in Paris that June and startlingly paraphrased Hofmannsthal when he wrote:

I have the feeling that Hofmannsthal begins each of his 'pastiches' of a past age with an ironic intention, but that his wonderful virtuosity brings them off so successfully that he always ends up by taking them seriously.

Though he could not know it, he was prophesying Helen's doom.

Fencing around the issue, Strauss delayed work on the second act. Composition of the *Parergon* (op.73) and collaboration with Hofmannsthal on a spectacle for Vienna based on Beethoven's incidental music and Kotzebue's epilogue, *Die Ruinen von Athen*, filled in the time; he also had slight involvement in the arrangement of music for a film version of *Rosenkavalier* in 1925. By that summer, *Die Aegyptische Helena* was little advanced and with the exception of a plea to Hofmannsthal to make the ending more poetical and less theatrical, he does not appear to have begged the kind of revisions he had sought in the past. Even a holiday in his beloved Greece and Italy failed to inspire him to the

116

Maria Jeritza, the most famous if not the first Helen, with Strauss shortly after the first performance in Vienna of *Die Aegyptische Helena*, 1928.

necessary heights and not until October 1927 was the score completed.

Then there were casting difficulties. Maria Jeritza would have been the ideal Helen (and so she was at the later Vienna performance), but her fees prohibited her presence at the Dresden première and the creators came close to blows over her substitute, Elisabeth Rethberg. Hofmannsthal the idealist rejected her as wildly unsuitable; Strauss the realist exerted himself to the limit in

117

diplomatic negotiation. He was infuriated when Hofmannsthal criticised his lack of success. He was tired of compromise, but he could do no better. Both in Dresden on 6 June 1928 and in Vienna five days later, the opera provided their first experience of outright failure.

Fritz Busch, giving his second Strauss première at Dresden, was hardly the ideal interpreter, markedly out of sympathy with music he criticised as superficial mood-painting (though he did remark that hearing the composer take up the baton for the first act during rehearsals was like encountering a different work). Strauss had inherited from Ritter the secret of maintaining a uniform symphonic tempo in each act of a Wagner opera, though he probably could not have done the same for Act 2 of *Die Aegyptische Helena*, with its convolutions of text and musical subject-matter, its phoney orientalisms, the dramatically unconvincing capitulation of the statuesque but static Helen, and the noisy, hollow gestures of the finale. In 1933 he collaborated with Lothar Wallerstein, the first producer of *Intermezzo*, in a revision of this act. It remains disjointed, but there is too much good music earlier in the opera to warrant neglect of the work as a whole. With a convincing dramatic soprano and her *lirico spinto* counterpart in the rôle of Aithra, the sumptuous shape and high profile of the vocal lines in Act 1 and Helen's monologue 'Zweite Brautnacht', which opens Act 2, can be highly effective. In that first act, Strauss and Hofmannsthal between them undertook a mythological spoof for the last time – and carried it off successfully.

Chapter 12

Compromise

When *Helena* seemed likely to founder in the Egyptian desert, Strauss turned his hopes towards the 'second *Rosenkavalier*' Hofmannsthal had promised him. In February 1927 he had completed another commission from the pianist Paul Wittgenstein, the Greek-inspired *Panathenäenzug*, and with the full score of *Helena* ready that autumn, his winter schedule was empty. Then Hofmannsthal came up with the proposition of combining sketches from his comedy about the popular Viennese Fiaker balls of the 1860s, *Der Fiaker als Graf* (The Cabby as Count) with the plot of *Lucidor*, a short story drafted back in 1909. In it a girl falls in love with her proud sister's suitor and wins him by the device (well precedented even by the time it appeared in Shakespeare's *Measure for Measure* and *As You Like It*) of taking the favoured lady's place in the suitor's bed. Operatically, the characters would be strongly contrasted. One sister could be a dramatic soprano, glamorous and brilliant, the other a *soubrette*, lighter and resourceful. A Croatian nobleman, as the successful lover of the older girl, would strike a breath of fresh air into the shabby social milieu – in itself a world away from the glittering Vienna of *Rosenkavalier*. Strauss liked this Slavic bonus, having toyed with Turgenev's *Smoke* as a subject, though the playwright's shift of interest from the younger to the elder sister (the Arabella of the opera's subsequent title) pleased him less. She was intended as a free-thinking specimen of the 'new woman', familiar to Hofmannsthal from Shaw and Ibsen, but to Strauss's mind she lacked the inner tensions of the Marschallin or Barak's wife.

As work proceeded in 1928, it was this problem which led Strauss to prompt greater dramatic incident and more finely honed psychological detail. He accepted that he would never have the telegrammatic manner of *Intermezzo* from the expansive Hofmannsthal, but this at least gave him a better chance of following the *cantilenas* and the sequence of set numbers which had become so heavily encrusted with Wagnerian echoes in *Helena*. Act 1 was excellent, he said, but it needed a more effective curtain – and as always he was to have it (in Arabella's pensive monologue 'Mein Elemer'). What Hofmannsthal proposed to follow, however, lacked the necessary conflict. He had invested what dramatic interest there was in the contrast between the relationship of the high-minded lovers and the background of an unscrupulous society on the make (diligently researched from an historical point of view and strikingly close in some ways to Vienna as he knew it in those profiteering post-war years). Even so, this opportunity for blending sentiment and satire was not enough for Strauss. He suggested that the placid happiness of Mandryka and Arabella at the Act 2 ball should be shaken by the groom-to-be's jealous misunderstanding of Arabella's innocent rôle in her sister Zdenka's scheme.

He went further – too far, perhaps – when he wrote to Hofmannsthal in the November, 'How would it be if that temperamental Mandryka, the minute Arabella is presented to him as unfaithful, were to shoot himself, and if Arabella then offered the glass of water [the Croatian-style acceptance of betrothal] to the dying man?' Hofmannsthal stayed calm; he felt that as soon as Strauss saw his proposals for the second and third acts, they could discuss at length the problems raised and all would be well. Strauss received the alterations to Act 1 in July 1929. On 14 July he sent a telegram to Hofmannsthal: 'First Act excellent. Many thanks and congratulations.' It arrived at Rodaun the following day, but Hofmannsthal never opened it. Two days earlier, his son Franz had committed suicide and the shock, added

Rehearsal for *Arabella*, 1933: Viorica Ursuleac as the heroine, Strauss advising Martin Kremer (the first Matteo).

Arabella at the Dresden State Opera, 1933, sets by Leonhard Fanto and Johannes Rothenberger. In the centre is Alfred Jerger, the first Mandryka.

to all his griefs and recent illnesses, was too much for him to bear. While dressing for the funeral he collapsed and died of a stroke.

Shielded so fiercely by Pauline that he had not even been permitted to attend Hofmannsthal's funeral a few days later, and still uncomprehending of the full extent of his loss, Strauss had the first act with which to pay fervent tribute, though inspiration of a kind lasted only until September. Then, faced with only the unrevised text of the rest of *Arabella*, he employed his capacity for hard work in a collaboration with Lothar Wallerstein on a new performing edition of Mozart's *Idomeneo*. This was another consolidation of a tradition which concerned him deeply, a labour of love which entailed rearranging much of the score, writing new recitatives and adding an interlude in Act 2 along with a final ensemble. He conducted the first performance in Vienna on 16 April 1931. Meanwhile *Arabella*, like her predecessor, hung fire. That Strauss ever completed the opera at all was probably due to a considerable amount of pressure from Dresden, where he had promised Fritz Busch the first performance. In the event the break in its composition was not as fatal as it had been for *Die Frau ohne Schatten* or *Die Aegyptische Helena*. Strauss still found some beautiful ideas for the mellifluous lovers' duet in Act 2 and for a serene closing scene where the glass of water, with just sentimentality, finds its target mercifully alive. The orchestration

Adolf Hitler with students of the *'Führerschule'* in 1933.

too, demonstrated his concerns for balance – expressed already in the *Intermezzo* preface – applied to more fulsome textures. But unsurprisingly the construction of both these acts remains considerably weaker than the first, as finely proportioned an act as any in the whole of the extraordinary Strauss-Hofmannsthal collaboration. Here, for Hofmannsthal's last lyrical return to comic realism, Strauss had found melodic impetus, transparent scoring, a duet and an aria (with assistance from Croatian folksong) as rich in sentiment and warmth, given the setting, as anything in *Der Rosenkavalier*.

By the time of the première, on 1 July 1933, another cloud had gathered. At the beginning of the year Adolf Hitler was appointed Chancellor of Germany and a month later his National Socialist party took control. The new party's promises of a stable economy and an impressive employment programme (in contrast to the

Weimar Republic's plunge towards catastrophe), and the finger it pointed at the Jews, long the scapegoats of European disaffection, seemed to many strong ointment for Germany's wounds. The almost immediate curtailment of cultural freedom was the first manifestation of a terrifying reality. Busch and the producer Alfred Reucker were dismissed from their posts at Dresden. Strauss had insisted that he would see *Arabella* through with them both, or not at all, but he was tied to the rules of his contract and found himself powerless to protest. *Arabella* went ahead with Clemens Krauss instead of Busch at the helm. It was the composer's first reluctant compromise with the new power.

On every previous occasion when politics interfered with his musical affairs, Strauss had survived by circumspection and lip-service. He had lived on as the serpent at the Kaiser's breast, mitigating the shocks of *Feuersnot* and *Salome* with a palatable diet

Stefan Zweig

of military marches and occasional pieces, and he must have thought he could do the same now. As far as he was concerned, the retrospectively distressing nationalism of the *Olympische Hymne* he composed in 1934 for the notorious games of 1936 signified no more than the pompous brassiness of the marches for the ceremonial *Feierlicher Einzug* written in 1909 for the Knights of the Order of St John, or the fanfares he had completed for Vienna more recently. In 1933, at least, Strauss was hardly alone in his largely untroubled optimism. Stefan Zweig, the Austrian novelist, biographer and playwright, explained in his autobiography, *The World of Yesterday*, how few people in a supposedly civilised Germany at that time had any conception of what could happen:

One cannot easily dispose of thirty or forty years of deep faith in the world inside of a few brief weeks. In the clutch of our conception of justice we believed that there was a German, a European, a world conscience and were convinced that there existed a measure of barbarousness that would make its own quietus, once and for all, because of mankind. Since I am trying here to stick to the truth as much as possible I have to admit that none of us in Germany and in Austria in 1933 and even in 1934 thought that even a hundredth, a thousandth part of what was to break upon us in a few weeks could be possible.

It is worth remembering that all the Nazi 'service' of which Strauss still stands accused (his music remains unplayed in Israel) took place in those early years. Much of it, too, had consequence for Zweig's short-lived safety as his new-found – and Jewish – librettist. Strauss was crucial as an establishment figure to the Nazis, and at this stage that meant tolerating his associates even if, like Zweig, they came from detested non-Aryan stock.

Zweig had been introduced to the composer through the

mediation of the publisher Anton Kippenburg. He was already well-known as the author of penetrating psychological biographies (much influenced by his admiration for Freud) and short stories; his outstanding, and only, full-length novel *Ungeduld des Herzens* (translated as Beware of Pity) came later in 1939. In Vienna he had been acquainted with figures from the musical world such as Reger and Busoni. Brought up in the same Viennese humanist tradition as Freud and Hofmannsthal, his work had always been imbued with a concern for moral values, and when he suggested a substantial adaptation of Ben Jonson's comedy, *Epicœne, or the Silent Woman*, Strauss realised that Zweig's approach to it would provide him with everything he needed in the way of sentimental satire and accepted the text without hesitation.

Like Rolland, Zweig took some time to penetrate the apparently inscrutable façade of the 68-year-old Strauss, but he found an immediate clue to the truth:

At first his face impresses as almost banal with its fat, child-like cheeks, the rather ordinary roundness of features and the hesitantly retreating brow. But only one glance into the eyes, those bright, blue, highly radiant eyes, and one instantly feels some particular magic behind this bourgeois mask. They are perhaps the most wide-awake eyes I have ever seen in a musican, not daemonic but in some way clairvoyant, the eyes of a man cognisant of the full significance of his task.

What Zweig seems not to have grasped is that only when a work fired him to the challenge did Strauss disclose the kind of immediate, 'clairvoyant' enthusiasm he recalled of their meeting. In fact the text of *Die schweigsame Frau* was the only one Strauss hardly altered – in thanksgiving, no doubt, at finding a man he believed to be Hofmannsthal's worthy successor. After Zweig had delivered the completed libretto to him on 17 January 1933, he worked at great speed, seeing the dramatic force of the situations in musical terms with extraordinary clarity.

At that time Ben Jonson was an unfamiliar figure even in Britain; on the Continent his name meant next to nothing. His corrosive, acerbic wit and cynical characters are tellingly back in favour today, though even now the razor-sharp edge of his wit does not quite atone for the relentless thrust of his most unlovable characters. Zweig, who discovered Jonson through a French history of literary England, rose to the challenge of humanising the harshness: the noise-abominating misanthrope of *Epicœne* gained a soft heart in *Die schweigsame Frau*, and Strauss perhaps felt he could afford more sympathy for this victim than he had cared to extend to the similarly beleaguered Ochs. The new motivation of the plot, too, suited him well: the 'silent woman', a

Strauss at work on *Die schweigsame Frau* (though the score of *Arabella* is on the piano).

disguised boy in Jonson, was transformed into the tender-hearted actress wife of the old man Morosus's unjustly dispossessed nephew, Aminta, and she feels a quite unJonsonian pity for her taunted uncle-in-law.

But while the framework of the action, brought forward to the eighteenth century, offered pastiche pastures new to the ever-inventive composer – matching the period with canzonas and ensembles in the sparkling tradition of Italian *opera buffa* – the core was apt to become over-sentimental. Morosus was given a great deal of music in which Strauss tried to lend him something of the nobility of Wagner's Hans Sachs, but its commonplace diatonic gestures fail to touch our hearts as they do Aminta's. One glimpse of the authentic Straussian warmth at the conclusion of the second act, as the lovers sing together while Morosus falls asleep in an adjoining room, points up the shortcomings of the Epilogue, when the old man observes, sententiously and out of character, 'how beautiful life is . . . when one knows how to live'. Strauss had first used this kind of harmonically straightforward musical language, almost Schubertian in its simplicity, in Sophie and Octavian's duet at the end of *Rosenkavalier*; it had worked

Strauss with his elder grandson Richard at Garmisch.

with the honest Barak in *Die Frau ohne Schatten* and there were moments to come in the last operas where it would play an undeniably effective part. Yet in *Die schweigsame Frau*, perhaps, it came too easily in the wake of Strauss's joy at finding his new collaborator.

The short score was ready by November 1933. Strauss worked on the orchestration throughout most of the following year and added the *potpourri* overture when all else was completed. Zweig found Strauss's easy-going eagerness to continue surprising in the light of the help he seemed to be offering the Nazis during 1933. Twice he stepped in to conduct: in March, when the Jewish-born conductor Bruno Walter was advised to withdraw from a Berlin Philharmonic concert, and for a performance of *Parsifal* at

Bayreuth in August, after Toscanini had refused to continue; on both occasions, as Strauss would naïvely explain, he was putting musical considerations before political advantage. This reasoning could not, however, be applied to the addition of his signature to the hysterical and declamatory ostracism of artists such as Thomas Mann and Hindemith, with whom he was personally acquainted. On 15 November Joseph Goebbels, in charge of the Nazi party's cultural decimations, appointed Strauss President of the *Reichsmusikkammer* without consulting him, and Strauss made no effort to resist the latest of what he afterwards described to Zweig, with patent contempt, as 'pestiferous honorary positions'; why should this be any different from his status with the Kaiser? But he had personal reasons for his apparent compliance, besides safeguarding the future of his new opera and librettist. Like Zweig, his daughter-in-law Alice, whom Franz had married on 15 January 1924, was Jewish; and his two grandsons, Christian and Richard, were thus half-Jewish. The ill-defined threat of the 1938 pogroms and the Final Solution already hung in the air.

Even in the early 1930s Strauss's association with Zweig was denounced as 'scandalous', though the score and libretto of *Die schweigsame Frau* were published and Strauss thought that a meeting with Goebbels in 1934 had given the work the seal of official protection. The first performance was planned for Dresden on 24 June 1935. Two days earlier Strauss saw that Zweig's name had been omitted from the programme and furiously insisted that it should be reinstated. It was, though the action cost the Dresden Intendant, Paul Adolph, his job. With the 41-year-old Austrian Karl Böhm conducting and Maria Cebotari, another soprano later to be celebrated for her Strauss rôles, as Aminta, the occasion passed successfully. There was a second performance, a third, and even a fourth before the Nazis silenced *Die schweigsame Frau* for a decade. On 17 June 1935, Strauss wrote a letter to Zweig. In it, he berated Zweig's 'Jewish obstinacy' and set out all too plainly his feelings about the compromises he had so far made with the régime and his own artistic creed:

Do you imagine I have ever been led in the course of a single action by the thought that I am Germanic (perhaps, *qui le sait*)? Do you suppose that Mozart was consciously 'Aryan' in his composing? For me there are only two sorts of people: those who have talent and those who haven't, and for me the People only begin to exist when they become the audience.

But the letter had been intercepted and on 6 July two Nazi officials came to Garmisch, proffering the offending material and demanding Strauss's resignation from the *Reichsmusikkammer*.

Only now did he begin to realise that a political power could wield such force over a mere musician. In a rare moment of despair the frightened old man wrote an obsequious apology to the Führer, explaining how he had always dedicated himself to the service of holy German art. In private he diverted his bewilderment with the salvation of work. Within the space of six years he had lost two collaborators whose verbal skill and poetry could inspire him, and he doubted if he could find another. Work with Zweig was now out of the question. All he could do was to take up Zweig's pressing advocacy over the last few months of a suitable substitute, and lose himself in the only world he knew.

Strauss and Josef Gregor, never the most relaxed of collaborators.

Chapter 13

Fable and Allegory

Josef Gregor was the man Zweig hoped could take his place as the new Hofmannsthal. A Viennese art historian and archivist, he had been briefed by his colleague over Strauss's continuing preoccupation with the spectacular *Semiramis* opera so often turned down by Hofmannsthal, so it was no mere coincidence that he visited the composer with the proposal of reconsidering it. That meeting, in April 1935, prompted no more than a curt dismissal from Strauss, and for the moment nothing came of it; then he still had high hopes for more from Zweig. At the 1934 Salzburg Festival – with which he had been associated since he first conducted Mozart there in 1922 and where he was now present to see Krauss conduct *Elektra* – he had met Zweig and they had discussed another theme which might stand as a humane plea in the midst of mad times. Zweig's pacifist ideals and Strauss's long-denied desire for a sixteenth or seventeenth century subject combined in a scheme based on the play *La Redencion de Breda* by Calderon de la Barca, the great Spanish writer whose work had influenced Hofmannsthal's last play, *Der Turm*, in 1925. The drama dealt with Spinola's capture of Breda in 1625 and his magnanimous pardon of the captives. Zweig proposed lending the action symbolic significance for Germany by transferring the action to the end of the most terrible period in the nation's history so far, the Thirty Years' War of 1618-48.

Zweig wanted to emphasise what he called the 'tragic, heroic and humane' elements, so it is curious to find Strauss expressing such pleasure in an action which would obviously entail the archetypal figures populating Hofmannsthal's later work for him, even if they would be set here in a more realistic context. Characteristically Strauss was soon wanting to inject the 'red corpuscles' of his most successful operas in the form of a love affair between the wife of the besieged town's commander and a lieutenant. 'I am afraid lest I can't summon up a melody which will touch the heart', he wrote to his librettist late in the summer of 1934, attempting to justify the element which Zweig found too bathetic. 'What I propose to you is, naturally enough, operatic – but where does kitsch stop and opera begin?'

Zweig, under increasing political pressure, had no chance to formulate a solution. Time after time he felt the threat of catastrophe which Strauss blithely ignored, at the same time urging Gregor on Strauss. When the blow fell with the *Die schweigsame Frau* première, the composer had little option but to let Gregor take over ostensible control while Zweig played the rôle of puppet-master behind the scenes. The day after the Nazi visit to Garmisch, Strauss saw Gregor again, skimmed in a matter of minutes through his six proffered sketches and absently selected three: the proposed continuation of the peace-opera (then entitled *1648*), a Greek bucolic subject and another which may well have been the germ of their third collaboration. His treatment of the diligent academic suggests that his notions of 'talent' expressed in the incriminating letter to Zweig found no place for the toleration of a mere 'schoolmaster', and the correspondence with Gregor, terse and cruelly to the point, states what the art historian's self-congratulatory reminiscences carefully neglect to mention. Work on the Calderon-inspired opera soon became wearisome to Strauss, and in a final, covert letter to Zweig in October 1935 (addressed to 'Morosus' and signed 'Storch') he thanked him for all he had tried to do, adding:

The whole material is after all a bit too everyday – soldiers – war – mediaeval heroism – people all dying together – it doesn't really suit me . . . I would have liked still a little joy in my work for the last years of my life . . . *Friedenstag* [Day of Peace, the opera's new title] is too wearisome a task – Gr.'s verses have no depth, they are nothing but nicely ringing surface tones without music.

Strauss rehearsing *Ariadne auf Naxos* at Covent Garden, November 1936.

Here ended Zweig's friendship with Strauss. He stayed in Vienna a year after the *Anschluss* and in 1939 he travelled to England. He and his wife died of massive veronal overdoses in Petropolis, Brazil, in February 1942, despairing that the world would ever see light at the end of the war.

Strauss proceeded, all the same with the score of *Friedenstag*, diverted only by a number of conducting tours, and it was completed on 16 June 1936. He believed that the first performance of this one-act work, his shortest since *Elektra*, could wait until he found a companion-piece for it, and he set to work on the second of Gregor's drafts, the Greek subject, almost immediately. The tale of Daphne, the virginal nymph, and her flight from the profane love of Apollo into the world of nature, would complement *Friedenstag* as another ode to peace, this time in a pastoral context, and both operas would end in celebratory choral cantatas. Gregor's dramatic sense in *Daphne* proved no more felicitous, as Strauss had lamented to Zweig when mulling over the elected scripts from that brief meeting: only more 'schoolmasterly' banalities, with the conflict between the 'colourless' Daphne and her suitors – the Sun God and the feminine shepherd Leukippos – being weaker in potential even than the original *donnée* of *Arabella*. But at least the matter was closer to Strauss's heart as he sat in the Garmisch study, looking out at the mountains and closing his ears to the increasing din of the Nazi menace. He made the suggestion that the virginal nymph should 'represent the human embodiment of nature itself touched upon by the two divinities Apollo and Dionysus, the contrasting elements in art', and he was able to guide Gregor towards a framework which, however schematic, could be effectively adapted to musical purposes.

When he found himself unable to move beyond a certain point, he had no qualms about humiliating Gregor by taking his problems to others. One new adviser was Clemens Krauss, now director of the Vienna State Opera as Strauss had hoped, who proposed that Daphne's metamorphosis into a laurel tree should take place on stage instead of merely being proclaimed in Gregor's dreary closing chorus. That took Strauss another year to conceive, but in the dazzling light of a Sicilian summer in 1938 he lent the orchestral tone-poem what he called, remembering Hofmannsthal, 'the miracle of transformation' (the choral cantata was resuscitated, with Gregor's assistance, for the Vienna State Opera Chorus in 1943).

Krauss applied pressure for *Friedenstag* as a central attraction in the 1938 Munich Festival and there it shared the evening of 24 July with Beethoven's *Prometheus* ballet music. On 15 October the authentic double bill took place in Dresden conducted by *Daphne*'s dedicatee, Karl Böhm. Böhm recalled that as the curtain fell Pauline, sitting in the front row, leaned over and kissed him, adding that he wouldn't get another since he was too sweaty. Her high estimation of *Daphne*, however, has only come to be shared recently; it has taken 48 years for the opera to be rehabilitated in Munich, and 49 for it to receive a staging in Britain. On neither occasion did it share the programme with *Friedenstag*, which, not surprisingly, fared even less well. The text of the peace-opera had singularly failed to stir Strauss to heroic heights – and little wonder, given the platitudes of Gregor's stolid celebrants. He wrote preposterously to Strauss of the musical apotheosis that 'the only real comparison I can find is the closing of the Ninth [Beethoven's]' and the answer was characteristically terse: 'I hope in your enthusiasm of authorship you do not overrate me.' Discussion about the quality of *Friedenstag* has often been obscured by admiration for its pacifistic intent under a despotic régime, but the parallel with *Fidelio* does it no service. Only in the human interest of the Commandant's wife (forbidden her liaison

Strauss in Greece, 1926.

but granted an aria with typically generous, soaring phrases) did Strauss touch the heart as he wished, and on a level of sheer invention, the stark harmonies and orchestration of the citizens' siege-misery at the opening of the opera added another element to the composer's vocabulary.

If *Daphne* affords any companion in the theatre – in an ideal, if impossible situation – it is surely *Elektra*. Lame as Gregor's verses undoubtedly are, Strauss was drawn beyond them to the bucolic theme: this was the chance for a serene return to the Greek classical calm as filtered through Winckelmann and Goethe, a Germanic conception against which *Elektra* had been such a bold antagonist. Strauss mirrored the difference by using a similar structure to point out the extremes in contrast between the myths. He fashioned an exquisite miniature prelude for woodwind where in *Elektra* Agamemnon's ghost had stood; as a chorus on this occasion he introduced tranquil shepherds calling across a Poussin landscape, followed as before by the entrance of the solitary heroine, who this time ponders on the beauties of nature rising from the orchestra, not the miseries of her degradation and shame. The careful contrast of dialogues and scenes through varied rhythms, tempi and scoring gives *Daphne* an almost symmetrical shapeliness akin to its sister opera. The orchestra in *Elektra* had been used with terrifying appropriateness for its theme, but never had Strauss employed it with such translucent magic and subtle poetry as can be found in *Daphne*. His heartfelt answer to a brutal world took the form not of abstract humanity in the mass but of a powerful antidote in nature-worship. As he had pointed out to Hofmannsthal during the First World War, he created violent, combatant music in times of peace and images of beauty for a troubled age. *Elektra* and *Daphne* stand, through the potent medium of myth, at the uncompromising extremes of this attitude.

Cheerful mythology had not yet made its exit. The scenario of a Danae opera, proposed by Hofmannsthal before *Helena* became the accepted choice, was printed, with Strauss's consent, in a literary magazine, *Corona*. In it Hofmannsthal had welded together two gold-fables – the story of Danae, mother of Perseus, visited by Zeus in a shower of gold, and the tale of Midas, whose golden touch became his bane – to point the moral that love comes before money. Danae, intoxicated by the wealth her divine lover's attentions promise, is then wooed by Midas on the king of the gods' behalf. He falls in love with her himself, and when the furious Jupiter (Hofmannsthal used Zeus's Roman name, basing his tale on Ovid) strips him of his gold, Danae learns her lesson: she chooses a life of blissful poverty with Midas.

Gregor later claimed that his own text on the Danae theme was among those presented to Strauss during the course of their 1935 meeting; but in 1938, Strauss needed a reworking of his old collaborator's ideas. The figure of Jupiter, no more than a numinous presence in Hofmannsthal, was now to play a crucial part, and the complications extended to a third act in which Jupiter learns to accept his renunciation of Danae. Once again Strauss turned to Krauss for help with a final scene, and Gregor was so mortified that he stayed away from the *Daphne* première. Strauss was past caring. He had begun to see that in the third act he had found a vital medium for his own farewell to beauty and, sure that this would be his last opera, he felt he had every right to be poetically indulged. This fantastical comedy to which he was to give some of his finest Mozartian pastiche and brilliant effects took on a deeper meaning, and he needed the kind of verbal exchanges and dramatic ideas which would compel him to profound results.

The notion that he was summarising his deepest spiritual values led him to disregard the relevance of *Die Liebe der Danae* to a baffling world. Halfway through its composition war broke out, and by the time it was completed on 28 June 1940, it was clear that this spectacular, baroque entertainment could not be lavished on war-torn Germany. Krauss, anxiously pleading for another first, met with the reply that the opera could not be entrusted to production until at least several years after the war. That the conductor eventually managed to extract a pledge for its première at the 1944 Salzburg Festival had much to do with his increasing value in the light of Gregor's continual blunders. So successfully, in fact, had Krauss resolved the apparent impasses of *Daphne* and *Danae* that Strauss now sought his help over another of Zweig's proposals, *Prima la Musica, poi le Parole*. The theme of the Abbé Casti comedy, already set to music by Mozart's rival Salieri, dealt with a question that had preoccupied Strauss since the confusions and counter-claims of the 'hybrid' collaborations with Hofmannsthal: which came first, words or music? Strauss felt that while he had made his emotional farewell with *Danae*, the intellectual preoccupation of this subject could amuse him in his last years. Gregor's attempts to provide a satisfactory libretto, in 1935 and again in 1939, failed to give him the elegant word-parrying he needed, so he turned to Krauss, who he believed was clever and respectful enough to help him write his own text. It would be a tactful move to tell the easily reconciled Gregor what Bahr had told Strauss in 1916 when *Intermezzo* was first considered: that his own idiom would suit him best. In this way Krauss's rôle could be minimised as far as Gregor was concerned.

These were the firm foundations of *Capriccio* in 1940. As it presented itself, Strauss thought he hardly needed a poet for dialectics, though he had requested 'a pretty and graceful action worthy of a Beaumarchais, a Scribe and a Hofmannsthal'; only the tenet of Casti's play was to remain. Settling on 1770 as a significant date for the opera's setting – with Gluck's operatic reforms as the background – composer and conductor engaged Hans Swarowsky, one of Krauss's disciples and also an authority on the late eighteenth century, to research historical detail. The acme of French sensibility, a Ronsard sonnet, could be used to favour poetic inspiration without too jarring a sense of anachronistic impropriety. Strauss had abortively discussed the possibility of his theme being approached from every angle, and he had even listed a few:

> First the words, then the music (Wagner)
> or First the music, then the words (Verdi)
> or Only words, no music (Goethe)
> or Only music, no words (Mozart)

To run their objectives simultaneously, Krauss and Strauss set themselves the difficult task of moulding symbolic figures (a poet, a musician, and a countess whose task as muse it is to reconcile them) to living characters (such as Gregor could never have provided) who would discuss the dilemma wittily in the manner of Oscar Wilde and Molière. A theatre director, with more than a passing resemblance to Max Reinhardt, and the entertainments of dancers and singers would move the debate into other fields.

Such a proposal needed impressive structural organisation, which Strauss, with his infallible sense of theatre, had always found easy. The argument, running continuously through the opera in the *parlando* style of the *Intermezzo* scenes, would be intensified in a huge central scene with an octet and nonet (using the skills in ensemble writing acquired in *Die schweigsame Frau*), all the characters expressing their divergent points of view. The essential vein of sentiment would be conducted in the scenes where poet and composer respectively declare their love for the countess, and in the final monologue where she toys with her options ('wouldn't that be a bit kitsch?' wondered Strauss, though he knew it depended on his music to transcend the situation). The director would have his say on fustian-flavoured spectacle in an elaborate aria at the height of the debate, servants would comment on the day's events like the harlequins and scaramouches of *Ariadne auf Naxos*, and even a prompt by the evocative name of Taupe ('Mole') would make an unexpected nocturnal appearance. Strauss maintained a joke over the lady's choice: as the text has it, words and music remain indissoluble, but the first say in the opera belongs to the composer's String Sextet and the last, before the

Two composers and a librettist: Strauss and Clemens Krauss with the first Flamand, Horst Taubmann, at a rehearsal for the 1942 première of *Capriccio*.

horn call that brings down the curtain, is a motif from the composer's love-song.

Work on *Capriccio* proceeded rapidly through 1940; the short score was ready by February 1941 and in the summer of that year Strauss completed the orchestration. The first performance was arranged with astonishing speed for those troubled times, thanks to Krauss's favourable standing with the authorities. If the composer now stood aloof and tacit in his disapproval of Nazi policy, Krauss had lost no time in ingratiating himself with the leaders to secure musical advantage. After the war, he argued, like so many others, that he had made a last stand for disintegrating cultural values – and it is astonishing that the festivals he directed continued for so long, as disasters accumulated for Germany in

135

the second part of the war; he also stated that he had used his position in Vienna to help many Jewish artists escape at the time of the *Anschluss*. Whatever the truth of the matter, it was his influence with Goebbels that set in motion a Strauss Festival in Munich during 1942, and there on 28 October *Capriccio* received its first performance with Viorica Ursuleac, the new Strauss *prima donna* and Krauss's wife, as the Countess.

The promised première of *Die Liebe der Danae* was to be part of the composer's 80th birthday celebrations. But by 1944 Germany's earlier victories had been reversed and the bombings became so severe that Goebbels finally banned all festivals. Krauss again used his position to persuade Goebbels that rehearsals for *Danae* in Salzburg that summer had surely gone far enough to warrant an indulgent exception. The Salzburg *Gauleiter*, too, proved sympathetic and after a frantic juggling of dates the dress rehearsal went ahead on 16 August, three days before the Culture Minister finally cancelled all further performances (in Austria and Germany the dress rehearsal, or *Generalprobe*, carried far more importance than in Britain or America; but this was a crushing blow nonetheless). The producer, Rudolf Hartmann, has left us with a touching picture of the composer, shattered and deeply disillusioned as he was by then, following the preparations for the unfulfilled première (it was not until 1952 that Krauss gave *Danae*

Clemens Krauss and Strauss in London, 1947.

a decent inauguration at Salzburg). The rich, resigned orchestral interlude before the last scene moved Strauss profoundly, and after the dress rehearsal he was found in his dressing room clasping the score, gesturing heavenward and saying, 'When I make my way up there I hope I'll be forgiven if I bring this along too.'

Questioned by Krauss over the possibility of another joint work, Strauss replied that the end of *Capriccio* was 'the best conclusion to my life's work in the theatre'. Even so there is no reason why this perfectly proportioned masterwork should so completely have eclipsed the finest pages of its immediate predecessor. Perhaps the misguided attitude which expects a composer's last word to be definitive is to blame. Strauss was wrong when he humorously added that it was only possible to leave one will: just as Shostakovich's last three String Quartets approach the question of death from so many plausible angles that we seek in vain for ultimate truth in the despairing Fifteenth, so in quite a different manner did Strauss explore the possibilities inherent in both his subjects without covering the same ground. *Danae* has its faults – a typically laborious text from Gregor, static characters and obscure motivation. Yet it also has a golden, serene atmosphere of its own which is no mere repetition of *Daphne*. Strauss saw it as a kind of 'Grecian *Götterdämmerung*' and, for all the light-hearted gestures of the opera, it is the figure of Wagner, having threatened to obtrude too heavily on Jupiter's wrath in Act 2, which treads lightly with the god in the airy, valedictory final scene. If *Capriccio* remains in some ways a world apart, these two amazingly fertile productions of a man in his eighties share an uncannily radiant exclusion of the questions of the time in which they were written. There was still time enough for grief and lamentation, but in the graver measure of a different medium.

Chapter 14

Quiet Curtain

It had been Strauss's habit even after his resignation from the Vienna directorship in 1924 to spend the winters with Pauline in their *Schlösschen* ('little castle') next to the Belvedere. At the outbreak of the Second World War they had to evacuate their Viennese stronghold, but life all the year round in Garmisch had become harder after the Zweig episode. The Nazis had proof of Strauss's contempt and, since Pauline made things worse by her outspoken remarks against the régime, Alice and the grand-children found themselves subject to increasing persecution. So when in 1942 the Intendant of Vienna, Baldur von Schirach, offered the family the city's hospitality and their old home there on condition that they made no further public blunders, it was necessary to agree. Those who criticise Strauss for not having emigrated like other musicians should consider two points. First, those others, with a few heroic exceptions, were Jewish; second, Strauss was nearly 80 years old. Otto Klemperer's facile remark that he stayed because Germany had 56 opera houses and America only two takes for granted the extraordinary number of conduct-ing commitments the aged and physically infirm composer was determined to honour.

As thanksgiving Strauss allowed the string sextet Introduction to *Capriccio* a preliminary airing at von Schirach's house that May. Strauss was an important figure in the Intendant's plans to maintain Vienna's cultural standards throughout the calamitous later stages of the war. That year, too, the Vienna Philharmonic celebrated its centenary and Strauss presented the orchestra with a sketch of a tone-poem he had taken no further; its subject was an Austrian equivalent to Smetana's *Moldau*, following the course of the Danube to the country's capital where its arrival would be celebrated by a choral cantata. He added a personal tribute: 'only he who has *conducted* the Vienna Philharmonic players knows what they are!' The following winter they recorded many of Strauss's orchestral works; all except the interpretation of *Symphonia Domestica* were lost in the subsequent bombings. Earlier record-ings, mostly from the previous decade with Berlin orchestras survive, however, to show us the fabulous textural clarity and cumulative force Strauss elicited from his players. Walter Legge described the former as 'a refutation of the charge which has so often been brought against him of overfilling his scores with detail'. He reported of performances Strauss gave in Dresden of the Mozart G minor Symphony, K.550, and his own *Don Quixote* and *Till Eulenspiegel* that:

While those who heard this concert still live, there will be testimony against any conductor who makes a Strauss work thick or fuzzy that, properly played, these works are as clear and transparent in texture as Mozart's.

Vienna remained for a while the civilised refuge it had proved after the First World War. This was a time for tranquil retrospection, for a musical reconnaissance of earlier years and with astonishing spontaneity Strauss produced in leisurely hours a second Horn Concerto and a Sonatina in F for Wind, commemorating his previous experiments in these forms – the Serenade for wind instruments (op.7) of 1882 and the 1883 Horn Concerto (op.11). He even dedicated the Sonatina, completed whilst convalescing from an illness in 1943 and subtitled 'From an Invalid's Workshop', to the players in Dresden whose predecessors had given the first performance of the 1882 Serenade. Both the later works, like *Capriccio* and *Danae*, blithely kept trouble or doubt at bay and although the harmonies mirror much that had passed since those respectable first exercises there is, if anything, a lighter touch; spring rather than autumn is in the air.

Forced to retreat from the bombing of Vienna in 1943, Strauss wrote the last bars of the Sonatina in Garmisch that summer. Then the disasters of war struck for the first time at the heart of his private world. On 2 October the Munich Nationaltheater was destroyed in an air-raid; Strauss told his sister Johanna he was speechless with grief. Worse was to follow. When the Nazis sought to requisition the Garmisch villa for the convalescence of war victims, Strauss turned them away with the curt reply that as far as he was concerned the war should never have taken place – 'on my account no one had to die'. For the second time he had set himself at risk; only the sympathetic intervention of a Nazi leader, Dr Hans Frank, prevented Hitler's wrathful actions from extending beyond the compulsory occupation of the servants' quarters in January 1944 and an edict forbidding contact between Strauss and the party commanders.

His fortification now was to immerse himself in a thorough reading of the complete works of Goethe – an act of faith in a German national humanity it was becoming impossible to believe had ever existed. This spiritual reserve did him some good. In September 1944 Goebbels closed down the opera houses, and when the final blow of the bombings of the Dresden and Vienna

Munich Opera House after
the bombing.

opera houses fell in 1945, the significance of losing the buildings
where he had enjoyed so many inaugural triumphs finally goaded
him to produce a response – *Metamorphosen*, an elegy for 23 solo
strings. The title referred not to the continous variations of the
work itself but to the term Goethe used in his old age to describe
his mental processes, and the parallel is reinforced by the
quotation from the poet's *Zähme Xenien* (Peaceful Epigrams)
found among the sketches for *Metamorphosen*. (From this source,
too, came the tiny epigram set to music in Strauss's last *Lied*
before the *Four Last Songs*, written in September 1942.) The
lines express the personal philosophies of two lifetimes, a quiet
determination, now become for Strauss a vital code of living, to
carry on regardless of circumstance. They are difficult to render
poetically in translation, but their gist is that no-one can fully
understand the strange workings of the world; better to know
yourself as best you can. Say to yourself, Goethe concludes, 'until
now all has gone well; so will it continue to the end'.

It was exactly this quest for continuing self-knowledge which
had led Strauss along his own path, regardless of other upheavals
in musical history, to the consistent and unique worlds of
Capriccio, the instrumental works of the forties and ultimately to
the *Four Last Songs*. In *Metamorphosen* he made one bewildered
effort to understand his feelings over the devastation of the world
around him. The result was a stern and sombre valediction
celebrating mourning in an almost ritual manner. In spite of a
familiar richness in the central fantasia, a florid remembrance of

140

things past, he left the inexorable chords of the funeral rites to triumph. They were dogged by the rhythms of the theme from the Funeral March second movement of Beethoven's *Eroica* Symphony, which Strauss claimed had risen unbidden from his unconscious mind before he made full and conscious use of it in a final quotation. He used a reverse sequence of hope and despair in the revised version of his 1939 concert waltz *München*, disrupting a pattern which included a glowing treatment of Kunrad's apostrophe to Munich from *Feuersnot* with a dissonant minor middle section of lamentation. *Metamorphosen* allowed no such optimism; like the concluding night of *Eine Alpensinfonie*, it left an implacable impression which, thus exorcised, would leave the way clear for more 'happy music'. Strauss completed *Metamorphosen* on 12 April 1945, though it had to wait until January 1946 for its first performance with Paul Sacher and the Zürich Collegium Musicum.

Germany's long expected defeat came finally at the end of April and American soldiers marched up the garden path to the Garmisch villa. 'I am the composer of *Rosenkavalier*. Leave me alone', Strauss told them, but that was not the end of it. One of the soldiers happened to be John de Lancie, principal oboist of the Philadelphia Orchestra, and the evening the two spent discussing matters musical brought forth some remarkable photographs which show the childlike enthusiasm of the old composer as he demonstrates passages from his most famous opera. Another lasting result of that meeting was the Oboe Concerto commissioned by de Lancie, extending the Mozartian possibilities of the Second Horn Concerto and providing the soloist with a graceful and substantial work in a sparse repertoire. It was another example of art concealing art: the oboist's seemingly spontaneous cantilena at the start of the work necessitated a taxing 46 bars without interruption. The orchestra, too, had a grateful contribution in a vein which approached the autumnal mood of the very last works.

Hounded by the Nazis during the later years of the war, Strauss now had to face a 'de-Nazification' tribunal which was to examine the implications of his heedless assistance back in the early 1930s. For the second time in his life he was penniless, his assets frozen in Germany. After a great deal of pressure, he and Pauline succumbed to the advice of friends and left Garmisch for Switzerland in October 1945. Though Pauline suffered from frequent illnesses and expressed her unhappiness in alarmingly regular arguments with domestic staff, her husband, it seemed, could work anywhere. As they moved from hotel to hotel he orchestrated the Oboe Concerto and in December 1947 completed another work just as blithe, if less well proportioned, the *Duett-Concertino* for clarinet and bassoon with strings and harp. In it he

Examining a painting in the Berne Art Gallery, Switzerland, 1947.

First flight: the 83-year-old composer arrives at Northolt Airport, 4 October 1947.

was remembering the long-standing devotion of the Vienna Philharmonic's principal bassoonist, Hugo Burghauser. The last instrumental piece to be completed at Garmisch shortly before their departure, a second Wind Sonatina, joined these works in a series of first performances around Switzerland.

Strauss also made several regrettable attempts – understandable in the light of his latest financial crisis – to raise money from his operatic successes. They included a 'waltz-sequence' from *Rosenkavalier* where he sanctioned no less than three cuts in the short Prelude, disposing the rest of the material in slipshod fashion, and a *Frau ohne Schatten* Fantasia using parts of the opera which, on his own avowal, he had found least satisfactory. The Fantasia was heard in London during October 1947. With Beecham's encouragement the British had offered Strauss a truce before the German tribunal could make up its mind and on

Strauss and Sir Thomas Beecham at a Drury Lane rehearsal.

4 October Strauss took his first journey by aeroplane to attend a London festival in his honour. Norman Del Mar, a horn player in Beecham's newly-founded Royal Philharmonic Orchestra, was entrusted with the conducting of the Fantasia and recalls in the Preface to his authoritative three-volume study of the composer how Strauss 'came up to the podium, glumly regarded the score for a few moments, muttered "All my own fault" and went away.'

Otherwise it was a triumphant celebration. At the same concert, on 5 October 1947, Strauss witnessed Beecham conduct *Don Quixote*, with Paul Tortelier making his English début as cellist, the *Bourgeois Gentilhomme* Suite and the *Feuersnot* Love Scene. For a second concert given a week later, the programme comprised *Macbeth*, the 'Christine' Interlude from *Intermezzo*, *Ein Heldenleben* and the final duet from *Ariadne* with Maria Cebotari and Karl Friedrich. Earlier that year and during the

Festival, Beecham recorded the *Bourgeois Gentilhomme* Suite and the operatic excerpts, and one of his two performances of *Elektra* for the BBC third programme, on 24 and 26 October, has also been released on record. Strauss's conducting contributions to the Festival included *Don Juan*, the *Burleske* and *Symphonia Domestica* with the Philharmonia at the Albert Hall, and *Till Eulenspiegel* with the BBC Symphony Orchestra just before he left at the end of the month. He had consolidated his friendship with Beecham and spent many hours looking at the paintings in the National and Tate Galleries and the Wallace Collection. The works of Titian, Tintoretto and Correggio were another reassurance, like his Goethe study, that civilisation remained intact in spite of what had happened. He told Willi Schuh of his old plans and sketches for an 'artists' symphony with Veronese's *Helen* as the theme of the Adagio. But no less important for his well-being were the handsome earnings from his visit which he took back to Switzerland.

Reunited with Pauline in their self-imposed exile, he was moved to one last inspiration by the words of the poem *Im Abendrot* by the German romantic poet Joseph von Eichendorff, whose evocative verses on the different times of day Strauss had used in a song-cycle for chorus and orchestra in 1928, *Die Tageszeiten*. The words of 'Im Abendrot', describing a couple looking into the sunset and asking with peaceful resignation, 'Is this perhaps death?', were so clearly and touchingly applicable to his situation that he set it as a song with glowing orchestral accompaniment in May 1948, while he and Pauline were biding their time in Montreux. Reflecting on the cycle of seasons and their application to the times of life in a book of poems by Hermann Hesse, and spurred on by his son Franz, he then decided to complement 'Im Abendrot' with four other settings. He eventually completed only three that summer: 'Frühling' (Spring), 'Beim Schlafengehen' (Going to Sleep) and 'September'. With clear-eyed sentiment he added characteristic autobiography, evoking the hero's withdrawal in *Heldenleben* through the horn coda of *September* and quoting the ideology motif from *Tod und Verklärung* for the last time.

Nor was death, when it came, so far from the epilogue he had long imagined. Yet in the year he still had to live, he accomplished much. In November he completed one more song, in the same nostalgic vein as the others but on a miniature scale and arranged for voice and piano. It was dedicated, like the *Vier letzte Lieder* ('Im Abendrot', 'Frühling', 'Beim Schlafengehen' and 'September'), to Maria Jeritza who kept the only copy of the song among her papers in America; only after her death in 1984 could *Malven*, to flower-verses by Betty Knobel, be reclaimed. A bladder infection troubled Strauss during 1948 and an operation

144

Strauss congratulating members of the Royal Philharmonic Orchestra.

was finally performed in Lausanne in December. Now that the 'deNazification' board had cleared him of complicity with the Nazis he and Pauline were free to return to Garmisch, but convalescence kept him in Switzerland until the following April. In June 1949 he managed to travel to Munich for his eighty-fifth birthday celebrations and even conducted the final scenes of Acts 2 and 3 of *Der Rosenkavalier*. For a special present he chose, perhaps surprisingly, a staging of the original *Ariadne auf Naxos* within Hofmannsthal's entertainment *Der Bürger als Edelmann*. He was awarded his third honorary doctorate, this time from Munich University (after earlier gestures from Heidelberg and Oxford). A month later he made his last visit to Munich to conduct the Moonlight Music from *Capriccio* for Bavarian Radio.

In August he suffered a series of minor heart attacks. Knowing the end was near, he 'produced' his own departure with touching aptness. On 29 August the producer Hartmann visited him and found him enfeebled but clear-visioned, still lamenting the losses of the opera houses in the war but full of hopes and fears for the future of the operatic tradition (he had set these out in full in a letter to Karl Böhm in April 1945). He also quoted to Hartmann, forgetting where it came from, Isolde's farewell to Brangäne in Act 1 of *Tristan*: 'Grüss mir die Welt' ('Greet the world for me'). 'I

145

In conversation with Ernst Roth and Henry Wood.

can hear so much music', he told his daughter-in-law, Alice. And when she asked if he wanted her to bring him some manuscript paper, he answered, 'Dying is just the way I composed it in *Tod und Verklärung.*' He died peacefully on 8 September. At his cremation four days later, the same three singers he himself had conducted earlier in the year in Munich sang the Trio from *Rosenkavalier.*

The couple who had held hands and gazed into the sunset were not separated for long. Pauline, deprived of her reason for living, died less than a year later on 13 May 1950, nine days before Kirsten Flagstad gave the first performance of the *Vier letzte Lieder* in the Royal Albert Hall with Furtwängler conducting the Philharmonia Orchestra. With this performance, Strauss achieved from beyond the grave a 'finale', as quiet and deeply moving as the kind of opera curtain that he had commended to Hofmannsthal: 'It is at the end that a composer can achieve his

In the audience at the Drury Lane Theatre.

finest results', he had told him of *Rosenkavalier*. He had not been wrong then and in a different manner he succeeded for the last time with the *Vier letzte Lieder*. There could have been no more consistent or dignified epilogue to the life of a man who maintained his sense of beauty to the end.

Conducting the Bavarian
State Opera Orchestra for his
85th birthday celebrations.

Catalogue of Works

Op.
1   *Festive March* for orchestra (1876); Munich, 26 March 1881
2   String Quartet in A major (1880); Munich, 14 March 1881
3   Five Pieces for piano (1881); no record
4   Suite in B flat major for 13 wind instruments (1884; originally Op. 15); Munich, 18 November 1884
5   Sonata in B minor for piano (1881); no record
6   Sonata in F major for cello and piano (1883); Nuremberg, 8 December 1883
7   Serenade in E flat major for wind instruments (1882); Dresden, 27 November 1882
8   Concerto in D minor for violin and orchestra (1882); Vienna, 5 December 1882 (version for violin and piano)
9   *Stimmungsbilder* for piano (1884); no record
10   Eight *Lieder* to texts from Gilm's *Letzte Blätter*: 'Zueignung' (orch. 1940); 'Nichts'; 'Die Nacht'; 'Die Georgine'; 'Geduld'; 'Die Verschwiegenen'; 'Die Zeitlose'; 'Allerseelen' (1883)
11   Concerto no. 1 in E flat major for horn and orchestra (1883); Meiningen, 4 March 1885
12   Symphony in F minor (1884); New York, 13 December 1884
13   Piano Quartet in C minor (1884); Weimar, 8 December 1885
14   *Wanderers Sturmlied* for chorus and orchestra to a text of Goethe; Cologne, 8 March 1887
15   Five *Lieder* to texts of Michelangelo ('Madrigal') and Schack ('Winternacht'; 'Lob des Leidens'; 'Aus den Liedern der Trauer No. 1'; 'Heimkehr') (1886)
16   *Aus Italien* (1886); Munich, 2 March 1887
17   Six *Lieder* to texts of Schack (1886): 'Seitdem dein Aug' in meines schaute'; Ständchen'; 'Das Geheimnis'; 'Aus den Liedern der Trauer No. 2'; 'Nur Muth!'; 'Barkarole' (1887)
18   Sonata in E flat major for violin and piano (1887); Munich, 3 October 1888
19   Six *Lieder* to texts from Schack's *Lotosblätter*: 'Wozu noch, Mädchen'; 'Breit' über mein Haupt'; 'Schön sind, doch kalt die Himmelssterne'; 'Wie sollten wir geheim sie halten'; 'Hoffen und wieder verzagen'; 'Mein Herz ist stumm' (1888)
20   *Don Juan* (1888); Weimar, 11 November 1889
21   *Schlichte Weisen* – Six *Lieder* of Dahn: 'All mein Gedanken'; 'Du meines Herzens Krönelein'; 'Ach Lieb, nun muss ich scheiden!'; 'Ach, weh mir unglückhaftem Mann'; 'Die Frauen sind oft fromm und still' (1888)
22   *Mädchenblumen* – Four *Lieder* of Dahn: 'Kornblumen'; 'Mohnblumen'; 'Epheu'; 'Wasserrose' (1886)
23   *Macbeth* (1890); Weimar, 13 October 1890
24   *Tod und Verklärung* (1889); Eisenach, 21 June 1890
25   *Guntram* (1893); Weimar, 10 May 1894
26   Two *Lieder* of Lenau; 'Frühlingsgedränge'; 'O wärst du mein' (1891)
27   Four *Lieder* to texts by Henckell ('Ruhe, meine Seele!' – orch. 1948), Hart ('Cäcilie' – orch. 1897) and Mackay ('Heimliche Aufforderung'; 'Morgen!' – orch. 1897) (1894)
28   *Till Eulenspiegels lustige Streiche* (1895); Cologne, 5 November 1895
29   Three *Lieder* to texts of Bierbaum: 'Traum durch die Dämmerung'; 'Schlagende Herzen'; 'Nachtgang' (1895)
30   *Also sprach Zarathustra* (1896); Frankfurt, 27 November 1896

31   Four *Lieder* to texts of Busse ('Blauer Sommer', 'Wenn'; 'Weisser Jasmin') and Dehmel ('Stiller Gang' – with viola obbligato) (1895-6)

32   Five *Lieder* to texts of Henckell ('Ich trage meine Minne'; 'Liebeshymnus' – orch. 1897; 'O süsser Mai'), Liliencron ('Sehnsucht') and from *Des Knaben Wunderhorn* ('Himmelsboten')

33   Four songs (*Gesänge*) with orchestra to texts of Mackay ('Verführung'), Bodmann ('Gesang der Apollopriesterin'), Schiller ('Hymnus') and Goethe ('Pilgers Morgenlied') (1896-7)

34   Two songs (*Gesänge*) for unaccompanied choir to texts of Schiller ('Der Abend') and Rückert ('Hymne') (1897)

35   *Don Quixote* (1897); Cologne, 8 March 1898

36   Four *Lieder* to texts of Klopstock ('Das Rosenband' – orch. 1897), from *Des Knaben Wunderhorn* (Für funfzehn Pfennige'; 'Hat gesagt – bleibt's nicht dabei') and of Rückert ('Anbetung') (1897-8)

37   Six *Lieder* to texts of Liliencron ('Glückes genug'; 'Ich liebe dich' – orch. 1943), Falke ('Meinem Kinde' – orch. 1897), Dehem ('Mein Auge' – orch. 1933), Bodmann ('Herr Lenz') and Lindner ('Hochzeitlich Lied') (1898)

38   *Enoch Arden* – melodrama for voice and piano to a text of Tennyson (1897); Munich, 24 March 1897

39   Five *Lieder* to texts of Dehmel ('Leises Lied'; 'Der Arbeitsmann' – orch. 1941; 'Befreit' – orch. 1933; 'Lied an meinen Sohn') and Bierbaum ('Jung Hexenlied') (1898)

40   *Ein Heldenleben* (1898); Frankfurt, 3 March 1899

41   Five *Lieder* to texts of Dehmel ('Wiegenlied' – orch. 1900; 'Am Ufer'), Mackay ('In der Campagna'), Liliencron ('Bruder Liederlich') and Morgenstern ('Leise Lieder') (1899)

42   Two choruses for male voices from Herder's *Stimmen der Völker*: 'Liebe'; 'Altdeutsches Schlachtlied' (1899); Vienna, 8 December 1899

43   Three *Lieder* to texts of Klopstock ('An Sie'), Bürger ('Muttertändelei' – orch. 1899) and Uhland ('Die Ulme zu Hirsau') (1899)

44   Two songs (*grössere Gesänge*) for low voice with orchestra to texts of Dehmel ('Notturno') and Rückert ('Nächtlicher Gang') (1899); Berlin, 3 December 1900

45   Three choruses for male voices from Herder's *Stimmen der Völker*: 'Schlachtgesang'; 'Lied der Freundschaft'; 'Der Brauttanz' (1899)

46   Five *Lieder* to texts of Rückert: 'Ein Obdach gegen Sturm und Regen'; 'Gestern war ich Atlas'; 'Die sieben Siegel'; 'Morgenrot'; 'Ich sehe wie in einem Spiegel' (1899-1900)

47   Five *Lieder* to texts of Uhland: 'Auf ein Kind'; Des Dichters Abendgang' (orch. 1918); 'Rückleben'; 'Einkehr'; 'Von den sieben Zechbrüdern' (1900)

48   Five *Lieder* to texts of Bierbaum ('Freundliche Vision' – orch. 1918) and Henckell ('Ich schwebe'; 'Kling!'; 'Winterweihe'; 'Winterliebe' – last two orch. 1918) (1900)

49   Eight *Lieder* to texts of Dehmel ('Waldseligkeit' – orch. 1918; 'Wiegenliedchen'), Remer ('In goldener Fülle'), Henckell ('Lied des Steinklopfers'), Panizza ('Sie wissen's nicht'), from *Des Knaben Wunderhorn* ('Junggesellenschwur') and from *Elsässische Volkslieder* ('Wer lieben will, muss leiden'; 'Ach, was Kummer', 'Qual und Schmerzen') (1900-1901)

50   *Feuersnot* (1901); Dresden, 21 November 1901

51   Two songs (*Gesänge*) for bass with orchestra to texts of Uhland ('Das Thal') and Heine ('Der Einsame') (1902, 1906)

52   *Taillefer*, cantata to a text of Uhland for sporano, tenor and baritone soloists, mixed chorus and orchestra (1903); Heidelberg, 26 October 1903

53   *Symphonia Domestica* (1903); New York, 21 March 1904

54   *Salome* (1905); Dresden, 9 December 1905

55 *Bardic Song* (*Bardengesang*) from Klopstock's *Hermannsschlacht* for three
  male choruses and orchestra (1905); Dresden, 6 February 1906

56 Six *Lieder* to texts of Goethe ('Gefunden'), Henckell ('Blindenklage'),
  Meyer ('Im Spätboot') and Heine ('Mit deinen blauen Augen';
  'Frühlingsfeier' – orch. 1933; 'Die heiligen drei Könige aus
  Morgenland' – orch. 1906) (1903, 1906)

57 *Two Military Marches: Militärmarsch, Kriegsmarsch* (1906-7); Berlin,
  6 March 1907

58 *Elektra* (1908); Dresden, 25 January 1909

59 *Der Rosenkavalier* (1910); Dresden, 26 January 1911

60 *Ariadne auf Naxos* – opera with play *Der Bürger als Edelmann* of Molière/
  Hofmannsthal (1912); Stuttgart, 25 October 1912
  Ariadne auf Naxos – revised version of opera with Strauss/Hofmannsthal
  Prologue (*Vorspiel*) (1916); Vienna, 4 October 1916
  Der Bürger als Edelmann – incidental music to the Molière/
  Hofmannsthal play (1917); Berlin, 9 April 1918

61 *Festive Prelude* (*Festliches Präludium*) for orchestra and organ (1913);
  Vienna, 19 October 1913

62 *Ein Deutsche Motette* to a text of Rückert for unaccompanied choir (1913);
  Berlin, 2 December 1913

63 *Josephslegende*, ballet (1914); Paris, 14 May 1914

64 *Eine Alpensinfonie* (1915); Berlin, 28 October 1915

65 *Die Frau ohne Schatten* (1917); Vienna, 10 October 1919

66 *Krämerspiegel*, song-cycle to texts of Kerr (1918)

67 Six *Lieder*: three songs of Ophelia from Shakespeare's *Hamlet* ('Wie
  erkenn' ich mein Treulieb?'; 'Guten Morgen, 's ist Sankt Valentinstag';
  'Sie trugen ihn auf der Bahre bloss'); three songs from Goethe's
  Bücher des Unmuts – Westöstlicher Divan ('Wer wird von der Welt
  verlangen'; 'Hab' ich euch denn je geraten'; 'Wanderers Gemütsruhe')
  (1918)

68 Six *Lieder* to texts of Brentano: 'An die Nacht'; 'Ich wollt' ein Sträusslein
  binden'; 'Säusle, liebe Myrte'; 'Als mir dein Lied erklang'; 'Amor';
  'Lied der Frauen' – orch. 1940 and 1933 (1918)

69 Five *Lieder* (*kleine Lieder*) to texts of Arnim ('Der Stern'; 'Der Pokal';
  'Einerlei') and Heine ('Waldesfahrt'; 'Schlechtes Wetter') (1918)

70 *Schlagobers*, ballet (1922); Vienna, 9 May 1924

71 Three Hölderlin Hymns for high voice and orchestra: 'Hymne an die
  Liebe'; 'Rückkehr in die Heimat'; 'Die Liebe' (1921); Berlin,
  9 November 1921

72 *Intermezzo* (1923); Dresden, 4 November 1924

73 *Parergon zur Symphonia Domestica* for piano (left-hand) and orchestra
  (1925); Dresden, 16 October 1925

74 *Panathenäenzug* for piano (left-hand) and orchestra (1928); Vienna,
  11 March 1928

75 *Die Aegyptische Helena* (1927); Dresden, 6 June 1928

76 *Die Tageszeiten* to a text of Eichendorff for male chorus and orchestra
  (1927); Vienna, 21 July 1928

77 *Five songs of the Orient* (*Gesänge des Orients*) to texts of Bethge: 'Ihre
  Augen', 'Schwung', 'Liebesgeschenk', 'Die Allmächtige',
  'Huldigung' (1928)

78 *Austria* to a text of Wildgans for male chorus and orchestra (1929);
  Vienna, 10 January 1930

79 *Arabella* (1932); Dresden, 1 July 1933

80 *Die schweigsame Frau* (1935); Dresden, 24 June 1935

81 *Friedenstag* (1936); Munich, 24 July 1938

82 *Daphne* (1937); Dresden, 15 October 1938

83 *Die Liebe der Danae* (1940); Salzburg, 16 August 1944

84 *Japanese Festival Music* (*Japanische Festmusik*) (1940); Tokyo,
  7 December 1940

85   *Capriccio* (1941); Munich, 28 October 1942
86   Divertimento after Couperin for small orchestra (1941); Vienna,
        31 January 1943

Other major works without opus numbers:

Burleske for piano and orchestra (1886); Eisenach, 21 June 1890
Lied to a text of Bierbaum: 'Wir beiden wollen springen' (1896)
Feierlicher Einzug der Ritter des Johanniterordens for brass and timpani (1909)
Dance-Suite after keyboard pieces by Couperin for small orchestra (1923);
    Vienna, 17 February 1923
Vienna Philharmonic Fanfare for brass and timpani (1924); Vienna, 4 March 1924
Olympic Hymn to a text by Lubahn for choir and orchestra (1934); Berlin,
    1 August 1936
Lied to a text of Goethe: 'Das Bächlein' (1933; orch. same year)
Die Göttin im Putzzimmer to a text of Rückert for unaccompanied choir (1935);
    Vienna, 2 March 1952
München, memorial waltz (first version 1939; revised version 1945); Munich,
    24 May 1939 (first version)
Two *Lieder* to texts of Weinheber: 'Sankt Michael'; 'Blick vom oberen Belvedere'
    (1942)
Lied to a text of Goethe: 'Xenion' (1942)
Concerto no. 2 in E flat major for horn and orchestra (1942); Salzburg, 11 August
    1943
Festive Music for the City of Vienna for brass and timpani (1943); Vienna, 9 April
    1943
Sonatina no. 1 in F major for wind instruments '*Aus der Werkstatt eines Invaliden*'
    (1943); Dresden, 18 June 1944
An den Baum Daphne for unaccompanied choir (epilogue to *Daphne*) (1943);
    Vienna, 5 January 1947
First Waltz-Sequence from *Der Rosenkavalier* (1944); London, 4 August 1946
Metamorphosen for 23 solo strings (1945); Zurich, 25 January 1946
Sonatina no. 2 in E flat major for wind instruments '*Fröhliche Werkstatt*' (1945);
    Winterthur, 25 March 1946
Concerto in D major for oboe and orchestra (1946); Zurich, 26 February 1946
Symphonic Fantasy from *Die Frau ohne Schatten* (1946); Vienna, 26 June 1947
Symphonic Fragment from *Josephslegende* (1947); Cincinnati, March 1949
Duett-Concertino for clarinet and bassoon with strings and harp (1947); Lugano,
    4 April 1948
Des Esels Schatten to a text of Gregor (1948; unfinished – completed Haussner)
Four Last Songs (*Vier letzte Lieder*) for soprano and large orchestra to texts of
    Eichendorff ('Im Abendrot') and Hesse ('Frühling', 'Beim Schlafengehen',
    'September') (1948); London, 22 May 1950
Lied to a text of Knobel: 'Malven' (1948)

Select Bibliography

Blaukopf, Hertha, ed.: *Gustav-Mahler-Richard Strauss – Correspondence 1888-1911* (London, Faber, 1984)

Beecham, Thomas: *A Mingled Chime* (London, Hutchinson, 1944)

Böhm, Karl: *Begegnung mit Richard Strauss* (Vienna, 1964)

Del Mar, Norman: *Richard Strauss: a Critical Commentary on his Life and Works* Three volumes (London, Faber, 1962, 1969, 1972)

Forsyth, Karen; *Ariadne auf Naxos: Genesis and Meaning* (Oxford University Press, 1982)

Gregor, Josef: *Richard Strauss: Der Meister der Oper* (Munich, 1939)

Hartmann, Rudolf: *Richard Strauss: The Staging of his Operas* (London, 1980)

Hofmannsthal, Hugo von: *Briefe der Freundschaft* (Frankfurt, 1953)

Jefferson, Alan: *The Operas of Richard Strauss in Britain, 1910-1963* (London, 1963) *Der Rosenkavalier*, Cambridge Opera Handbooks (Cambridge University Press)

John, Nicholas, ed.: English National Opera Guides to *Der Rosenkavalier* (No. 8) *Arabella* (No. 30), *Salome/Elektra* (No. 37) (London/New York, Calder/Riverrun)

Kennedy, Michael: *Richard Strauss* (*Master Musicians*) series (London, Dent, 1976)

Lehmann, Lotte: *Singing with Richard Strauss* (London, Hamilton Press, 1964)

Mahler, Alma: *Gustav Mahler: Memories and Letters*, edited by Donald Mitchell and Knud Martner (London, Sphere 1900 – fourth revised edition)

Mann, William: *Richard Strauss: a Critical Study of the Operas* (London, 1964)

Marek, George R.: *Richard Strauss: the Life of a Non-hero* (London, 1967)

Puffett, Derrick: *Salome* and *Elektra*, Cambridge Opera Handbooks (Cambridge University Press, 1989)

Rolland, Romain and Strauss, Richard: *Correspondence, Diary and Essays*, edited and translated by Rollo Myers (London, Calder and Boyars, 1982)

Schuh, Willi: *Richard Strauss: A Chronicle of the Early Years 1864-1898*, translated by Mary Whittall (Cambridge University Press, 1982)

Schuh, Willi: *Über Opern von Richard Strauss* (Zürich, 1947)

Specht, Richard: *Richard Strauss und sein Werk* (Leipzig, 1921)

Strauss, Richard: *Briefe an die Eltern* (Zurich, 1954)

Strauss, Richard: *Betrachtungen und Erinnerungen*, edited by Willi Schuh (Zurich, 1949), English translation by L. J. Lawrence as *Recollections and Reflections* (London, Greenwood, 1953)

Strauss, Richard: *Briefwechsel mit Hans von Bülow* (Bonn, 1953)

Strauss, Richard: *Briefwechsel mit Joseph Gregor* (Salzburg, 1955)

Strauss, Richard: *Briefwechsel mit Hugo von Hofmannsthal* (Zurich, 1952), English translation (with omissions) by H. Hammelmann and E. Osers (Cambridge University Press, 1980)

Strauss, Richard: *Briefwechsel mit Clemens Krauss* (Munich, 1964)

Strauss, Richard: *Briefwechsel mit Willi Schuh* (Zurich, 1969)

Strauss, Richard: *Briefwechsel mit Franz Wüllner* (Cologne, 1963)

Strauss, Richard: *Briefwechsel mit Stefan Zweig* (Frankfurt, 1957)

Wilhelm, Kurt: *Richard Strauss persönlich* (Munich, 1984), English translation by Mary Whittall (London, Thames and Hudson, 1989)

Zweig, Stefan: *Die Welt von Gestern* (Stockhom, 1944), English translation by Cedar and Eden Paul as *The World of Yesterday* (Cassell, 1944, 1987)

Acknowledgements and References

Acknowledgements are due for quotations from the following sources:

H. Blaukopf, ed., trans. E. Jephcott: *Gustav Mahler-Richard Strauss – Correspondence 1888-1911* (London, Faber, 1984); *Boult on Music* (London, Toccata Press, 1983); N. Del Mar: *Richard Strauss: A Critical Commentary on his Life and Works* Three volumes (London, Faber, 1962, 1969, 1972); H. Hammelmann and E. Osers, trans.: *The Correspondence between Richard Strauss and Hugo von Hofmannsthal* (Cambridge University Press, 1980); W. Legge: *On and Off the Record* (London, Faber, 1982); Lotte Lehmann: *Singing with Richard Strauss* (London, Hamilton Press, 1964); R. Myers, ed.: *Richard Strauss and Romain Rolland: Correspondence, Diary and Essays* (London, Calder and Boyars, 1968); H. Pleasants, trans.: *Eduard Hanslick: Music Criticism 1846-49* (London, Gollancz, 1951); W. Schuh, trans. M. Whittall; *Richard Strauss: A Chronicle of the Early Years* (Cambridge University Press, 1982); W. Schuh, ed., trans. L. J. Lawrence *Strauss: Recollections and Reflections* (London, Greenwood, 1953); S. Zweig: *The World of Yesterday* (London, Cassell, 1943).

In addition, I would like to thank Nicholas John, the late Kurt Lowy, Robert Matthew-Walker, Naomi Saxl and Isabel Morgan for assistance, reminiscences or helpful suggestions.

Index

(Illustrations are indicated by **bold** type)

156